Failed Stone

To my children: Galvin, Carly and Liam
May the buildings that house you in
the future benefit from the experience
gained from buildings in the past.

Patrick Loughran

Failed Stone

Problems and Solutions with Concrete and Masonry

Birkhäuser – Publishers for Architecture
Basel · Berlin · Boston

We would like to thank the Graham Foundation for
Advanced Studies in the Fine Arts for their generous
support of this publication.

"When I was a little boy.....
I used to walk by the beach and move stones
Just so there would be some residue of my existence,
Some change in the world
that resulted from my having been there."

Richard Solomon, 2002 speech
Director of the Graham Foundation from 1993–2005

Table of Contents

Preface

Terra-cotta blocks netted over to prevent from falling to the streets, Mather Tower, Chicago, 1928.

page 7 Concrete structure of Rhône-Alpes TGV Station at the Lyon Airport, 1994.

In the spring of 2002, I wrote a book entitled *Falling Glass: Problems and Solutions in Contemporary Architecture.* The research for *Falling Glass* helped me understand how glass failures could be avoided and enlightened me as to which innovations were being explored within the glass industry. Originally, the book was to include the investigation of a variety of building materials. Ria Stein, the book's editor, encouraged me to concentrate on glass with an offer to investigate other materials in future publications. *Failed Stone* represents a continuation of my research on building materials, specifically concrete, masonry, and stone.

To the untrained eye, the cover photo of this book appears to be a wonderfully textured material creating a basket weave appearance. To people familiar with façade design, the image shows the stone cladding of a world-renowned project, Finlandia Hall in Helsinki, designed by architect Alvar Aalto. The bowed panels were not part of the original design, but the effect of thermal hysteresis on flat white marble from Carrara, Italy. The panels deformed to an un-repairable state just 10 years after completion of the project, requiring the complete re-cladding of the entire building at a cost of more than 3 million euros. As I initially researched this project, I had an understanding that the façade problem had been repaired in a similar fashion to many other buildings throughout the world.

White marble buildings had become notorious failures that were being re-clad with metal and granite façades. I was shocked to find out that Finlandia Hall was re-clad with the same material that originally failed: thin white marble panels from Carrara. Incredibly, the photo on the cover is not of the original building, but of the replacement panels just a few years after installation. This architectural tragedy reminds me of a quote from George Santayana, an American philosopher and poet, "Those who cannot learn from history are doomed to repeat it."

The mission of *Failed Stone* is to present knowledge from past projects in an effort to prevent the occurrence of future problems. As *Falling Glass* described the limitations of glass in façade design, *Failed Stone* provides a guide to better understanding concrete, masonry, and stone. By sharing the lessons learned from great works like Finlandia Hall, my hope is to enhance the art of building. I am fortunate to practice architecture in Chicago, a city rich in architectural history. Chicago's great architectural past can come at a price. Turn-of-the-century buildings constructed with corroding carbon steel connections represent a hazard to pedestrians at the street level. Loose terra-cotta fragments have fallen to the street requiring many of our walkways to be sheltered with protective scaffolding. These older terra-cotta buildings are not the only masonry element with problems. More recent developments in masonry, such as the mortar additive "Sarabond", have brought about catastrophic building corrosion failures throughout the world. What at the time seemed like an innovative new product turned out to be an admixture which has been blamed for brick walls falling off of the face of new buildings. Although I believe there are lessons to be learned regarding the use of new products on large-scale projects, my intention is not to discourage the pursuit of innovation. On the contrary, I hope to encourage it through shared information.

As the subtitle suggests, this book is not all about the problems, but also the solutions. The architectural community is on the cusp of breaking tradition with materials that have

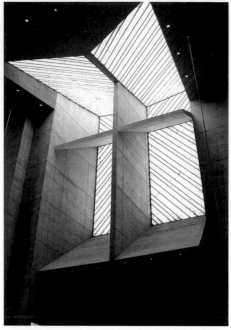

above The translucent marble façade is prone to vandalism and breakage. E.N.S.A.D. – Ecole Nationale Supérieure des Arts Décoratifs, Paris.

right Translucent stone façade allows light into the building. E.N.S.A.D., Paris, 1997

been used for centuries: concrete, stone, and masonry. Innovations with concrete in particular have pushed it to the forefront of architectural design solutions. Today architects are using concrete in revolutionary new ways. Superplasticizers are added to mixtures to keep concrete fluid during pours. Fiber reinforcement technology has abandoned the limitations of steel rebar structures. The possibilities of concrete seem endless. We photoengrave our concrete to bring it to life. We add copper aggregate to give it a natural green patina that changes with time. The industry has even developed a concrete mix that is translucent to allow light into concrete spaces. The use of modern concrete has allowed for

the creation of amazing structures like the Rhône-Alpes TGV station at the Lyon Airport; however, the collapsed precast panels at the Terminal 2E at the Charles de Gaulle International Airport in Paris are a sober reminder that concrete has limitations.

Stone has traditionally been used in massive sections to enclose our churches allowing stain glass to bring light inside. Today modern cathedrals such as Our Lady of the Angels in Los Angeles use exposed colored concrete to form its thick walls and $1\frac{1}{2}$ cm ($\frac{5}{8}$ inch) thick alabaster stone to bring light into the church. Ironically, these stone panels are protected on the outside by glass, reminding designers that as stone becomes thin, it also becomes weak. The E.N.S.A.D. – Ecole Nationale Supérieure des Arts Décoratifs façade shows the limitations of thin stone. The Paris school is composed of a translucent marble curtain wall. A fine layer of marble is laminated to the glass of a traditional curtain wall system. The fabrication of these glass and stone units requires the exterior stone surface to be polished down to a very thin layer in order to improve light transmittance. The building's stone appearance has been challenged by people throwing rocks from the street which penetrated the stone façade. Other stone façades have followed the E.N.S.A.D. project with the hope of resisting much more severe attacks. The Israeli Foreign Ministry Building provides a beautiful stone façade designed to resist bombs. The façade

Terra-cotta panel façade,
designed by Goettsch Partners,
Hessel Museum, CCS Bard
College, New York, 2006.

has challenged that perception with masonry structures that are light and fluid. His buildings celebrate the ingenuity of a great designer who was not limited by Uruguay's construction materials or labor force. Similar to brick, the use of terra-cotta is experiencing a re-birth in modern architecture. Many architects had abandoned terra-cotta as an old fashion decorative element prone to corrosion problems in buildings from our past. Architects such as Goettsch Partners have given this traditional material a dynamic new life in modern architecture with terra-cotta panels designed to resist weather and corrosion.

Part of the credit for these advances in concrete, stone, and masonry goes to new technologies from the construction industry and part goes to the imaginations of the architectural community. This publication serves not only to educate architects, educators, and students on the principles of concrete, stone, and masonry design, but to foster the pursuit of new ideas within the construction industry. The projects discussed in this book were developed by some of the greatest architects of the 20th and 21st centuries. They are innovative, creative designs. With any new creative endeavor comes the possibility of flaws and in some cases the possibility of "failed stone". This book describes many of the problems behind today's contemporary façade designs and offers possible measures designers can take to prevent problems. Each chapter of the book focuses on a particular mode of failure. The introduction of the chapter will discuss the fundamentals of the problem. Specific building examples will follow with explanations of how the type of failure can be detected. The end of each chapter will conclude with recommendations as to what could have been done differently to eliminate or minimize the risk of failure.

While this is a book about failures, it is not about liabilities, and the issue of whose fault these failures were remains deliberately undiscussed. The intention was not to determine responsibilities for past mistakes but to help avoid similar problems in the future.

of the reception hall includes panels so thin that the wall lights up like a lantern at night. The onyx panels are more than beautiful. They have been designed with spring clip connections tested for blast design. Today's stone enclosures can provide both light and protection to the inhabitants within.

Designers are transforming materials of the past like masonry into materials of the future. A traditional perception of brick is that of a building tool used for heavy-looking buildings with straight lines. The work of Eladio Dieste

Thermal Hysteresis

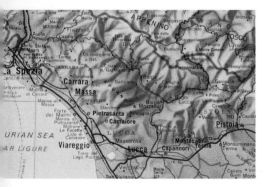

Approximately 100 kilometers (60 miles) west of Florence, Italy, is a city called Carrara in the province of Tuscany. Well known around the world for its white marble quarries, Carrara has provided its stone for such famous historic projects as the Trocadarro in Rome and the Marble Arch in London. In recent history, the white marble became infamous in modern architecture for being a failing cladding material for a number of contemporary large-scale projects. The stone failures have been attributed to a phenomenon known as thermal hysteresis.

Hysteresis is the changed response to an object due to a given influence, which leaves

above Carrara, in the province of Tuscany contains some of the most famous stone quarries in the world, known for their white marble.

center Like the imprint of a hand pushed in hard clay, thermal hysteresis can leave a physical history of forces applied to a material.

right Interior Carrara marble finishes at Amoco Building have not changed.

page 11 Amoco Building, Chicago, completed in 1972, had a history of stone problems related to thermal hysteresis.

a permanent record of how the object was influenced. For example, if one were to push a piece of clay it will assume a new shape, and when the hand is removed the clay will not return to its original form. The clay provides a physical history of the forces that have been applied to it.

Carrara white marble, exposed to large temperature variation, can suffer from the effects of thermal hysteresis. The effect can transform a flat piece of thin white marble into a dish-like form. The distortion is due to higher temperatures and differential thermal cycles from front to back of the panels, which results in different magnitudes of expansion. Simply put, as the stone is exposed to temperature variation it transforms its shape and never returns back to its original form. Like the clay example, thermal hysteresis permanently deforms the shape of the white marble. In addition to a change in the stone's appearance, thermal hysteresis includes a significant degradation of material strength. Over time the thin marble panels not only dish outward in a convex manner, they also become significantly weaker in flexural strength. Over years of thermal cycling, the stone panels can degrade to the point of becoming a block of loose granular material. Although the effects of thermal hysteresis on white marble have been known since the 1920s, the dangers of it became painfully evident in the 1970s when thin white marble panels installed on various towers around the world began to fail.

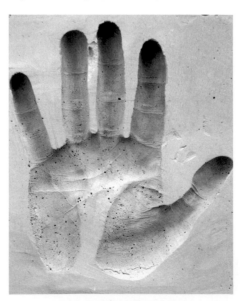

Mock-up of original Amoco Building façade at Construction Research Laboratory in Miami, Florida.

In the late 1960s, the Amoco Company embarked on the design of a new corporate office building in Chicago. The building design was developed as an 80-story tower like no other. It was to be one of the tallest buildings in the world. The Amoco Building had a unique exterior skin design with chevron shaped steel columns clad in white stone at the perimeter of the building. The triangular sections of the columns contained the bulk of the mechanical services such as the utilities and air-conditioning piping, thus permitting flush window walls inside the building. The plan allowed for a column-free space between the exterior wall and the center core. The design provided exceptional views of the city and Lake Michigan. Business executives in

research on the stone was completed. Representative samples of the selected marble were tested for flexural strength before and after exposure to thermal cycling. Testing indicated that a minimum flexural strength of 9.65 MPa (1,400 psi), incorporating the maximum anticipated strength loss of 40 percent due to thermal cycling, should be used for the project. A full-scale mock-up test was conducted in Florida at Construction Research Laboratory for wind and water intrusion as well as structural testing of the glazing and stone suspension system. This mock-up was used to test the assembly as a whole as well as to provide a visual review of the details prior to starting construction of the actual building.

At the conclusion of the design and testing phase of the project, 44,000 pieces of Alpha Gray marble from Carrara, Italy, were used to clad the perimeter columns of the Amoco Building. The work was completed in 1972. The average stone size was 127 x 107 x 32mm (50 inches high by 42 inches wide by $1\frac{1}{4}$ inches thick), except for the reentrant corners where the thickness of the panels was increased to 38mm ($1\frac{1}{2}$ inches) from the 42nd floor and above. The increased stone thickness at these locations was to compensate for the higher anticipated wind loads at the upper corners of the building. The marble panels were supported by 152mm long (6 inches) stainless steel bent plates connected to galvanized angles that were stud bolted into the structural steel chevron shaped columns. The marble panels had kerfs cut into them to receive the stainless steel bent plate. The downturned tabs of the bent plate provided lateral support for the stone below and the upturned tab provided lateral/bearing support for the stone above. Each piece of marble was independently supported back to the adjacent steel column. After installation, all of the joints between the marble panels were filled with sealant.

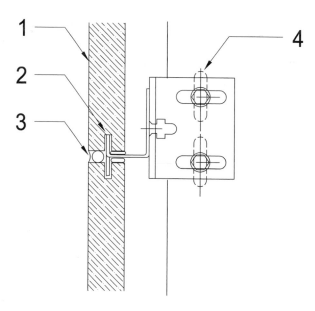

Section through marble connection
1 Marble panel 3cm or 4cm ($1\frac{1}{4}$–$1\frac{1}{2}$ inches)
2 Stainless steel bent plate
3 Backer rod and sealant
4 Galvanized steel angle connection back to chevron shaped steel column

the building could not fight over corner offices, because there were none. The tower's design incorporated a reentrant corner that made all of the perimeter offices the same.

During the design phase of the project, the selection of the stone to clad the building was not made lightly. In 1970, six Italian marbles were examined. Three samples of each marble were tested. Selection of the stone considered appearance, strength, and availability. The Carrara Alpha Gray marble was preferred based primarily on color. Prior to fabricating the stone cladding, extensive testing and

In 1979, inspection of the building indicated crescent shaped cracks in approximately 230 marble panels. The observed crescent shaped cracks occurred in the panels at the 152mm long (6 inches) stainless steel lateral connection points. Between 1979 and 1985, the

Inspection of the building indicated crescent shaped cracks were visible on the stone panels that clad the chevron shaped steel columns. Amoco Building.

below Stone panels are cut into blocks at quarry and can vary in physical properties depending on which part of the quarry they are extracted from.

building owner observed additional cracking and bowing of the marble panels. Outward displacement of the marble panels was found to be as much as 28.6mm (1⅛ inch). The outward bowing of the panels was actually an outward dishing of the stone, because the bow occurred along the vertical and horizontal axis of the panels. The effects were linked to thermal cycling, because approximately 80 percent of the significantly bowed panels were located on the south and east elevations of the building, which unlike the west elevations had no adjacent structures to block direct exposure of the sun. The marble panels on the north elevation of the building, which received the least amount of direct sunlight, had the least amount of outward bowing. As a result of these observations, a more thorough investigation of the building cladding began.

In 1985, laboratory testing was started to better understand what was happening to the stone. 96 marble panels were removed from the building and tested together with 10 original stone panels that had been stored in the basement of the building. The results of the laboratory flexural strength tests were startling. The minimum flexural strength of the virgin original marble panels was 7.52 MPa (1.09 ksi). This was much less than the minimum flexural strength of 9.65 MPa (1.4 ksi) gathered from initial test samples of the stone prior to construction. This proved that the stone used on the building was not as strong as the stone used during the preliminary sample testing for the project. This realization provided a painful reminder that stone strengths can vary in a quarry and that testing of stone samples during a large project needs to take

Elevation of straps used to
temporarily restrain the marble
panels. Amoco Building.
1 Panel and strap above
2 Bolt
3 Marble panel
4 Theoretical crack location
5 Stainless steel straps
6 Panel and strap below

right Temporary strapping
detail
1 Stainless steel bolt
2 Stainless steel straps painted white
3 Existing backer rod and
sealant
4 Existing marble panel
5 Existing galvanized angle
connected back to structure
6 Existing stud weld connection to stainless steel plate

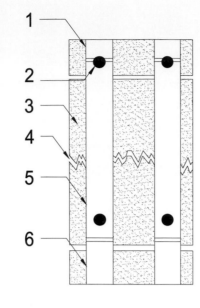

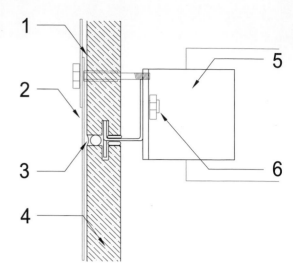

The granite blocks from the
quarry were tested during the
fabrication process. If results
were below minimum specifications, the blocks were
rejected.

place throughout the construction process.
Additional testing of the marble
panels removed from the building indicated
an average flexural strength of 5.24 MPa
(760 psi). This revealed a 40 percent loss in
strength compared to stone stored in the
basement. Through accelerated weathering
testing it was anticipated that in another ten
years on the building, the marble panels
would lose a total of about 70 percent of their
original strength. This would bring the average
flexural panel strength down to about 3.65
MPa (530 psi), and a minimum flexural
strength on the stone would be as low as 1.96
MPa (285 psi).

As the inspections continued, it became clear
that the cracking and dishing of the marble
panels on the building were accelerating at a
rapid rate. The deterioration of the stone panels made them unable to withstand anticipated wind loads. The test data was supported
by in-situ load tests of 48 actual full panels on
the building where a uniform negative wind
load was simulated with hydraulic rams at the
back of the panels. Rams were temporarily
installed on the exterior wall by removing
adjacent stone panels.

Although no stone panels had fallen off the
building, the strength loss to the panels
showed no sign of stopping, making repair
options futile. Based on these findings, it was

decided to remove the marble panels from the
building. Stainless steel straps, color coated
white to match the marble color, were bolted
through the marble into the supporting angles
to prevent any failing stone from coming off.

A variety of design solutions were considered
to replace the marble. However, the consen-
sus was to maintain the existing white image
of the tower. This decision suggested three
alternate re-clad materials: white aluminum
panels, white granite panels, and a man-made
ceramic glass. Based on a variety of factors
including appearance, cost, availability, and
established track records for cladding material
on high-rise buildings, a 38mm (1½ inch)
Mount Airy granite, quarried in North Carolina,
was selected for the re-cladding. Samples
from Mount Airy granite blocks were tested
during the fabrication process, and if results
were below minimum specifications the quarried blocks were rejected.The final connection
of the granite back to the existing structure
was very similar to the original detail. For
strength and corrosion resistance, a continuous stainless steel shelf angle was used to
support the stone in lieu of 152mm (6 inch)
kerfs. The angle was extruded to improve
connection tolerances.

In September 1991, approximately 20 years
after the tower was built, removal and replacement of all of the original 44,000 panels was

Calcite Crystals

Marble primarily consists of calcite crystals. Calcite crystals are anisotropic. Anisotropic means that when the stone is heated the crystals expand in different amounts in different directions, and when the stone is subsequently cooled, the crystals cannot return to their original position because they interlock. This phenomenon often results in a permanent expansion of the marble, increased absorption rate, and an accompanying strength loss. With large thermal cycles, some marbles can transform into very fine sugar-like particles through granulation.

In the case of some thin white marble panels, if the outside face of a panel is heated to a higher temperature than the inside, the outer face of the panel will expand more than the inside face. This explains the dishing out of the panels. On a building constructed in a northern climate, it is not surprising that panels facing north will have the least amount of dishing. These panels receive the least amount of thermal exposure on the exterior face of the stone. Although white marbles have been used for centuries in architecture, two factors have led to the dramatic effects of thermal hysteresis on contemporary buildings: the stone thickness and the climate.

Flexural strength of marble panels at Amoco Building

Condition	Original design samples for building	Actual panels installed on building	Difference
Original strength	9.65 Mpa (1.4 ksi) Minimum	8.69 MPa (1.26 ksi) Average	——
		7.52 MPa (1.09 ksi) Minimum	22% less than specified
After aging	5.79 MPa (840 psi) (40% loss)	3.65 MPa (530 psi) Average	——
		1.17 MPa (170 psi) Minimum (90% loss)	80% less than specified

above The Pantheon stone walls were constructed with 1.2m (4 feet) thick stone blocks. The stone panels that enclosed the Lincoln Bank of Rochester, New York, were 25mm (1 inch) thick.

complete. The vast majority of the removed panels were ground into pebbles for use as landscaping material, or donated to groups that manufacture small stone items. In order to better comprehend what happened to the stone on the Amoco Building, one must understand the composition of marble.

Stone Thickness

The first factor in understanding how hysteresis affects our modern buildings is to consider the evolution of stone in the history of construction. In early times, large blocks were used for the construction of buildings. The Pantheon completed in Rome in 125 A.D. was built with 1.2m (4 feet) thick stone walls and 1.9m (6 foot 2 inch) diameter solid stone columns. During the Medieval (9th through 15th century) and Renaissance periods (15th through 16th century) the use of solid blocks of stone in walls was converted into stone-faced walls consisting of random stone rubble set in a mass of mortar between inner and outer faces of stone ashlar. With the advent of skeleton steel frame construction in the late 1800s, the use of thick load-bearing walls evolved into

The desire to reduce the weight of cladding elements was linked with improved stone fabrication equipment in the 1960s to produce thin stone panels to skin our building.

above The 48 swooping columns were re-clad with aluminum panels. A total of 13,000 panels were individually computer-designed and fabricated to fit onto the existing metal framework.

right The re-cladding of the Lincoln Bank of Rochester, New York, originally completed in 1970, required a lightweight solution that would not add excessive weight to the existing metal support framing and building structure.

page 16 The Lincoln Bank of Rochester was clad with thin marble panels, fixed to a complex metal cage work.

thinner non-load-bearing walls. The Empire State Building, towering over 300m (1,000 feet) in the air was constructed in 1930 with wall thickness measured in inches and not feet. More than 5,600m³ (200,000 cubic feet) of limestone and granite were cut into panels and connected back to the steel structure. As our buildings reached to greater heights, it became very important to reduce the weight of cladding materials. The lighter the cladding material, the less steel structure would be required to support it. Building designs were aggressively trying to reduce the stone thickness of façades in order to reduce building costs. When the cladding wall or curtain-wall design principles were combined with improved stone fabrication equipment and techniques in the 1960s, the result was the start of 3cm (1 ¼ inch) thick stone panels to skin our buildings.

Around this time, the Lincoln Bank of Rochester, New York, wanted to provide its city with an elegant tower clad in expensive stone. The 20-story building design had a square plan with columns at the perimeter that fanned out at the street level on all four sides. The Lincoln Bank Tower was completed in 1970 using Carrara marble to clad the 48 swooping columns. Because of the building's unique form, the stone panels varied in width and height. The original design considered 5cm (2 inch) thick stone and connected to two-story-high steel cages, which were to

hang alternatively from the external columns of the building's structural frame. The final design was revised to 2.5cm (1 inch) thick panels hung from one-story-high cages, which were much lighter than the original design. Unfortunately, the fate of the Lincoln Bank cladding was similar to the Amoco Building in Chicago. Within 10 years of completion, the thin stone panels were dishing outward, requiring a full replacement. Unlike the Amoco Building, Lincoln Bank decided to re-clad the columns using lightweight aluminum in lieu of heavier granite material. Because of the unique shape of the building, the retrofit of aluminum panels required a total of 13,000 panels, which were individually computer-designed and fabricated to clad the 48 columns by Antamex, a Canadian-based curtainwall company. No two of the panels were identical. The demise of the Rochester Bank and Amoco Tower cladding was linked to the thickness of the stone as well as their climatic conditions. This leads to the second contributing factor which is thermal cycling.

Thermal Cycling

The second factor contributing to hysteresis, thermal cycling, is linked to the use of a southern-based building material in an unsuitable (northern) climate. As the calcite crystals in white marble transform with temperature

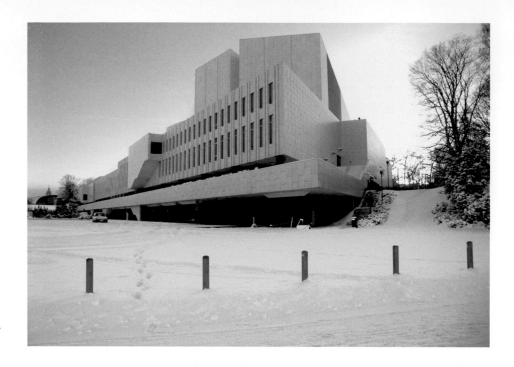

The government officially protected Finlandia Hall in Helsinki in 1993, declaring that the exterior should be kept "equivalent to the original".

The re-clad Finlandia Hall remains stark white as compared to the neighboring hotel re-clad in white granite.

page 19 above Finlandia Hall was constructed between 1967 and 1971 using white Carrara marble with a distinctive stone veining pattern rising diagonally from the panels.

below Finlandia Hall. Photo of bowing replacement panels taken in the winter of 2006.

this monumental building was not indigenous to the northern lands of Finland. The designers wanted this performing arts building to have a direct link to Mediterranean culture. Not by accident, the cladding material selected was from a quarry in the Apennine Mountains above Carrara, Italy. The marble cladding had a maximum panel size of 140cm and was 3cm thick (55 x 1 ¼ inches). Each panel was fixed by four pins. The pins were inserted 35cm (14 inches) in from the edges. Thus each panel was connected to four adjacent panels, overlapping at half the panel height. Similar to the Amoco Tower and the Rochester Bank building, the marble skin of Finlandia Hall was doomed to failure.

variation, stone panels can change from flat plates to round dishes. It appears that the greater the temperature differential on the stone, the greater the effect on the panels. In no project was this more evident than in the use of Italian marble in the northern climate of Helsinki, Finland.

Finlandia Hall was constructed between 1967 and 1971. The main part of the building rises like a white tower with inclined roofs. The design of the large volume above the auditorium was intended to improve the acoustics by providing a resonance space above the seating area. The cladding material used to cover

In July 1991, safety nets were hung along the length of Finlandia Hall to protect pedestrians from potential cladding failures from above. Similar to other projects, the stone panels on the north face did not suffer from the same dishing as panels on the east, west, and south. What is unique about Finlandia Hall is not the problem, but the solution. The government officially protected Finlandia Hall in 1993, declaring that the exterior should be kept "equivalent to the original". The appearance of the marble was required to resemble the original stone, even down to the pattern of the stone veins rising diagonally from the left to the right on the panels.

In 1997, re-cladding of Finlandia Hall with white marble was started. Work was completed in May 1999. In total, 7,000m² (75,320 square feet) of panels were replaced at a cost of over 3 million Euros. In autumn 2001, just three years after Finlandia Hall had been re-clad, it was realized that new panels were bending. Measurements have shown that the renovated walls of Finlandia Hall have deteriorated. The reduction in the strength of the marble since the slabs were replaced is 20–30 percent. Panels installed in autumn 1998 are bowed more than those installed the following spring. The reason for this can be attributed to the cold winter in Finland in 1998–99. The story of the cladding at Finlandia Hall demonstrates the irrational loyalty a community can have for great works of architecture.

David's replacement. Michelangelo's David, carved from a solid block of white Carrara marble, was moved indoors after being exposed to the elements for over 300 years.

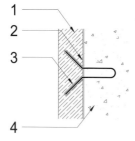

General Motors Building, New York City, 1968. Clad with white marble, with no signs of thermal hysteresis.

below Marble slabs supported by precast concrete panels similar to the ones used for the General Motors Building.
1 Marble veneer panel
2 Impervious isolation sheet
3 Stainless steel pin in drilled holes
4 Precast concrete panel

1
2
3

4

How Can Thermal Hysteresis Be Avoided?

The history of the famous Renaissance masterpiece David may shed some light on how thermal hysteresis can be avoided in white marble. In 1464, the Overseers of the Office Works (Operai) made plans to commission a series of twelve large Old Testament sculptures for the buttress of the cathedral of Santa Maria Del Fiore in Florence. Two sculptures had been created by Donatello and his assistant Agostino de Duccio, and they planned to create a David for the project. A large marble block, more than 5m (17 feet) tall, was carved from a quarry and Agostino began to shape the legs, feet and chest of the figure. For reasons unknown, Agostino's association with the project ceased with the death of his master Donatello in 1566, and Antonio Rossellino was commissioned to take up where Agostino had left off. Shortly thereafter, Rossellino's contract was terminated, and the large block of marble lay dormant, exposed to the elements, in the yard of the cathedral workshop for 25 years. In 1501, a young Michelangelo, only 26 years old, was given the contract to complete the massive biblical hero. He worked on the project for a little more than three years, prior to its unveiling in front of the Palazzo Vecchio on Piazza della Signoria. Although the sculpture had a reputation of being of poor quality, it remained there until 1873, when it was moved indoors to the Academmia gallery in Florence. How could the sculpture of David be left exposed to the elements for over 300 years with no signs of thermal hysteresis? The re-cladding of Finlandia Hall showed visible deterioration after less than three years. Obviously, the climate of Florence has far smaller thermal cycles than the streets of Helsinki; however, a closer examination of the stone will also reveal a difference.

The veining of the marble at Finlandia Hall was a prominent feature of the stone. The original stone as well as the replacement stone had a distinctive pattern with veins rising diagonally from the left to the right on the panels. The grain size of David is far less visible to the eye. The fine grain size is the most distinct property of the marble used for David. Studies suggest that the grain texture, veining and clear contours produce lower strength and prove less durable than slightly veined marbles. The stone used to create David had very little grain as opposed to the stones used on the architectural projects discussed. Have there been examples of white marble on buildings that have not failed? The answer is yes, and the successful projects are linked to unique installation techniques and quarried white marble stone with special material properties.

Installation Techniques

Installation techniques can contribute to the success of white marble on buildings. In the late 1980s, stone-faced composite panels, consisting of 5mm ($^1/_5$ inch) thick stone panels adhered to 4cm (1 $^1/_2$ inch) honeycombed aluminum, fiberglass, or sheet steel core began to be used on the exterior walls of buildings. An early example of this innovative technique using Carrara marble was completed at the new hall at the Fiera in Carrara. The building design required lighter loads than could be obtained with traditional 3cm (1 $^1/_4$ inch) panels. This led to the decision to use thin marble, 4mm ($^3/_{16}$ inch) thick, bonded to a honeycomb backing which tests have proven to be surprisingly resistant to flexure, even after frost treatment in an aggressive environment.

Another project that has had success with thin white marble in a northern climate is an office building in the town of Karjaa, which is west of Helsinki. The building was completed at about the same time as Finlandia Hall, with its façades made from Carrara marble. There is no visible evidence of dishing on this building. Many would speculate that the façade used material much thicker than the 3cm (1 $^1/_4$ inch) used at Finlandia Hall. In truth, the material is thinner. Similar to the hall at the Fiera in Carrara, the façade is made of composite panels consisting of 1cm ($^3/_8$ inch) thick stone with a 3cm (1 $^1/_4$ inches) concrete back-up system. The marble slab was pre-bowed by sandblasting the back of it until there was 4mm ($^3/_{16}$ inch) of bowing prior to attaching to the concrete substrate. As the concrete panel shrank with drying, the stone slab was straightened. Lastly, the General Motors Building in New York City was successfully clad with white marble in 1968. The perimeter hexagonal columns of this 50-story building were covered with domestically quarried 2.2cm (⁷⁄₈ inch) thick Georgia white marble connected to precast concrete panels. To date, the building has not experienced the severe affects of thermal hysteresis. The General Motors Building stands as a reminder that not all white marble cladding is the same.

Stone Testing

In order to predict which stones will suffer the effects of hysteresis, laboratory-simulated accelerated weathering testing is used to estimate the loss of strength in materials as a result of exposure to the weather. This issue is still being debated in the stone industry. There are critics that believe that durability (accelerated weathering) test procedures have no relationship to natural weathering. There is wide diversity between the durability test procedures preferred by the European Countries and freeze thaw testing used in the United States.

What is important to remember is that extensive testing was completed for the Amoco Building. However, the decision to use a building material that lost 40 percent of its strength due to freeze thaw cycling was still made. Testing alone will not avoid the problem. What the Amoco project lacked was a historic example/precedent of thin 3cm (1¼ inch) white Carrara marble installed on metal framing in a northern city. They desired to use a Mediterranean stone on a large-scale project without confirming its suitability for the Chicago climate. Amoco was not a small Italian Villa constructed of marble blocks; it was an 80-story office tower with a steel structure located just off the shores of Lake Michigan in Chicago. It can be dangerous to borrow design elements from buildings of the past without including the construction methods or climate considerations from which they came.

1

Stone is a natural material, and by its very nature is prone to material property variation. Marbles have an enormous range in initial strength properties and vary considerably in weathering characteristics. It is important to verify that the materials supplied to the site meet the project design requirements. The flexural strength of the marble supplied and installed on the building should not be less than the minimum specified flexural design strength. This occurred at the Amoco project. Quality control testing of the actual material being supplied should therefore be undertaken to ensure continued compliance with the required strength as calculated from design.

2

The use of thin marble panels on buildings in the late 1960s was relatively new, and therefore the in-service behavior of this type of stone on buildings had no history. The use of thin marble panels has led to complete façade replacement on several large-scale projects throughout the world. If stone is used in an exterior application for a large project, it is advisable to select a stone that has performed well over time in a similar circumstance.

3

If loss of material strength (hysteresis) is a concern, and if stone panels are going to be exposed to large temperature variation, material testing of stone should include accelerated weathering tests.

4

In keeping with the history of the use of stone in architecture, the thickness of stone used for exterior walls on buildings has been reduced substantially. The most dramatic decreases from 10.2cm (4 inches) to 3cm (1¼ inches) occurred during the last 40 years. Extensive research on material properties, including durability, must parallel the advancement in fabrication techniques. Large-scale projects must consider the ramifications of technical advancements prior to embarking on innovative installation techniques.

5

Marble has been successfully used as a building material for hundreds of years, and as a consequence its general physical properties and in-service behavior are known. However, the successful historical use of marble was based upon its being utilized in thick blocks or as thick panels of about 10.2cm (4 inches) or greater in bearing type walls. The Amoco Building used 3cm (1¼ inch) thick, non-load-bearing marble panels.

6

Not all marble claddings are alike. The General Motors Building in New York utilized thin stone panels to clad its tower, but selected domestic marble and a different anchoring system than Amoco to secure the panels to the structure. The General Motors building has not required re-cladding.

Stone faced composite panels with a thin layer of stone adhered to a honeycombed aluminum core has proven to be resistant to flexure, even after frost treatment in an aggressive environment.

Impact

People have the perception that brick, concrete and stone walls are impenetrable. This perception comes from historic buildings constructed with solid masonry walls 30cm (12 inches) in thickness. World War II bunkers were constructed with concrete walls measured in feet and not inches. Today's modern construction rarely uses this type of wall assembly. Concrete structures have become much thinner with innovative ultrahigh performing concrete and fiber reinforcement sys-

tems, sometimes less than 2.5cm (1 inch) thick. Masonry construction has moved to non-load-bearing veneer walls comprising a 9.21cm (3 $^5/_8$ inch) wythe with stone cladding panels typically 3.18cm (1 $^1/_4$ inch) in thickness, or sometimes thinner. Designers have to anticipate how building materials are going to be used and misused. Careful consideration must be made toward maintaining material finishes. Everything, from luggage to shovels, will dull sharp edges. A building element adequately designed to resist a uniformly distributed wind load can fracture due to the large concentrated load of a shopping trolley or skateboard.

Some types of structures have historically been at risk to blast effects because of the nature of what is inside them. For example, a grain-processing facility can be at risk due to the concentration of the combustible grain dust particles. Or a chemical plant can be at risk because of the volatility of the compounds it produces. Today, buildings are at risk due to terrorism. In a fraction of the time it takes to blink an eye, the impact of 4,000 pounds of explosives in a parked car can destroy the face of a building. The impact of bombs has become a force to be considered in many façade designs. Building hardening has

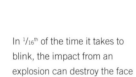

In $^1/_{16}$ th of the time it takes to blink, the impact from an explosion can destroy the face of an entire building.

A grain-processing facility can be at risk to blast effects due to the concentration of the combustible grain dust particles.

page 23 Stand-off distances can be achieved by installing bollards or planters around the perimeter of buildings. Blue Cross Blue Shield of Illinois Headquarters, Chicago, 1997.

right and below Murrah Building, Oklahoma City. Façade destruction due to impact.

moved into the forefront of enclosure design. As we move to designing against bursts of force, the criteria for acceptability have evolved. While breakage is allowed, safety of life is the priority. The design goal relates to structural redundancy, ductility and preventing progressive collapse. For Americans, the classroom for many of these concepts was in the town of Oklahoma City at the site of the Murrah Federal Building bombing.

On April 19, 1995, the Alfred P. Murrah Federal Building was destroyed by a truck bomb. The truck, which carried thousands of pounds of explosives, was located less than 3m (10 feet) from the front of the building. The Murrah Building and site proved to be ill prepared for this type of impact. The bombing forced the United States Government and America to rethink how its government buildings should be designed against acts of terrorism, and concrete and stone were part of the solution. Following the Murrah Federal Building collapse, three major design considerations have been developed for buildings of higher-level security: maintaining stand-off distance to a building, preventing progressive collapse to a building structure, and minimizing debris mitigation.

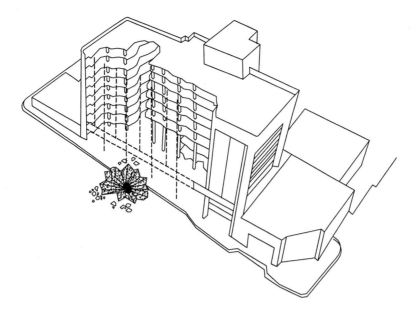

The Murrah Building destruction came from a truck filled with 4,000 pounds of explosives parked less than 3m (10 feet) from the face of the building.

Stand-off Distance

The intensity of a bomb blast is much higher near the detonation of the blast and dramatically reduces with distance away from this point. The first criterion to consider in designing new federal buildings was to prevent unwanted vehicles accessing a defined safety corridor around the structure. This is achieved by locating the building away from access roads, and providing barriers to prevent unauthorized vehicles from coming close to it. There are many elements of blast design that will almost surely be unpredictable, including the nature, location and intensity of the blast. Given this, it is unlikely that even the most rigorous design concept could ensure that structural damage could be prevented. The second consideration is to prevent a progressive collapse.

Progressive Collapse

When the nine-story Murrah Building collapsed, 168 people were killed. It has been estimated that a least 80 percent of the deaths were caused by the structure collapsing on occupants who might have otherwise survived the bomb blast. The Murrah Building's concrete structure was adequately constructed for traditional building loads. It was designed to resist forces from wind, snow, people and everything normally found in a building. It had not been designed to resist an explosion at its doorstep. In response to the Murrah Building collapse, several structural design changes have been incorporated into the design of federal buildings for the United States Government. In simple terms, blast design allows local structural damage to occur but designs against progressive collapse. This can be achieved through redundant design and ductile material behavior. For example, if a column were damaged or even eliminated in an explosion, what would this do to the structure?

The Murrah Building had a transfer girder running across the face of the structure at the second floor, which transferred the weight of ten building columns to five columns down to the ground. The failure of one column meant three failed; with the failure of two, as many as seven could fall. Localized damage is expected in a bomb blast; however, by preventing progressive collapse, designers hope to limit damage and save lives. In blast design sufficient redundancy must be available in all major structural elements, including beams, girders, columns, and slabs. All are to assume the loads carried by adjacent damaged or removed elements. Post-damage resistance is typically provided by the cantilever or caternary action to hold the damaged zone in place to facilitate rescue efforts. Transfer girders are less likely to be used in this type of design because they increase the potential for a catastrophic failure.

Designers are asked to put a greater emphasis on the overall ductile behavior of a structure in response to blast loading. Steel is the most probable material to consider, because by its very nature it is ductile. Steel bends and deforms elastically prior to failing. If a building were not designed for blasts, a traditional steel frame would perform better than concrete because steel has equal capacity in tension and compression, whereas concrete has capacity only in compression.

For example, in a simple reinforced concrete beam not designed for blasts, reinforcement only penetrates the supporting columns for a determined number of inches based on the length of the span. To resist normal

Construction of stone barrier wall at Oklahoma Federal Campus Building, Oklahoma City.

right Stone barrier wall mock-up, Oklahoma Federal Campus Building.

below Stone barrier wall close-up view.

right The stone barrier wall at the main entrance
1 Form tie voids to be grouted solid
2 25 x 25mm (1 x 1 inch) steeel mesh
3 15.2 x 15.2cm (6 x 6 inch) welded wire fabric (wwf) secured to form ties
4 Stone
5 Structural cast in place concrete wall
6 Grout

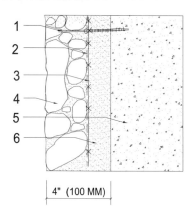

4" (100 MM)

the columns would not resist the outward movement of the columns, giving a second mode of catastrophic failure. With little or no reinforcement of concrete in the top of the beam or inadequate reinforcement penetrating the columns, the frame would fail. With additional reinforcement, it has a chance of staying in place.

Concrete structures can be designed for blast by using continuous reinforcement to tie the building together vertically and laterally. By doing this, there are alternative load paths implicit within a design. The alternative path method makes it possible for loads within a building to be redistributed when individual members are damaged or removed. This type of design can be implemented even if the exact nature of the threat is unknown. For example, if internal columns are accessible to the public but cannot be approached by vehicles, they can be made sufficiently robust to resist the threats delivered by individual suicide bombers.

Debris Mitigation

The fragmentation and propulsion of building components pose a great threat to life. Using architectural elements and systems that do not fragment during an explosion can remove this threat. Flying projectiles can cause as much harm as the explosion. New blast designs understand this, incorporating special frames and laminated glass to resist the force of an explosion without dislodging. If exposed to a blast, this type of glazing system will break; however, it will stay in one piece in its specially designed frame. Debris mitigation must be considered in all elements of a project, including the solid walls that surround buildings.

Blast Design

Shortly after the attack on the Murrah Building, the United States Government began reviewing its design criteria to incorporate blast requirements and other security measures in its buildings. The facility to replace the Murrah Building was to symbolize the strength and accessibility of the United States

loading, the majority of the steel reinforcement would be located near the bottom of the beam section (the tension zone) with the upper little or no reinforcement near the top (the compression zone). If a blast were to occur below such a simple reinforced concrete frame, the resulting force would push the beam up and possibly push its supporting columns outward. The upward force on the beam reverses its reinforcement needs causing it to lose its structural integrity and fail catastrophically. The short lengths of reinforcement penetrating

Front entrance to the Oklahoma Federal Campus Building, 2004.

The ground floor plan of the Oklahoma Federal Campus Building provides a perimeter of bollards and a stone wall at the main entrance to protect the face of the building.

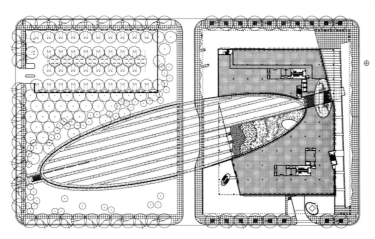

Government. The goal of the design was to look strong but not be oppressive. Security measures were to be transparent because the new federal building in Oklahoma City was to be open to the public as before.

The building structure would be one of the first new federal office buildings requiring blast protection. Designed by the architectural firm of Ross Barney + Jankowski, the Federal Campus Building in Oklahoma City is a 16,815m² (181,000 square foot) office building occupying the southern block of a two-block site. The site topography influenced the design of the building in such a way that the east wing of the building is three stories in height while the west side is four. To allow as much daylight as possible into the heart of this large floor plan, a large elliptical courtyard was incorporated into the design. A large window,

1.5 x 3.35m (5 x 11 feet), in the concrete walls, enabled the building interior to receive a good deal of natural sunlight.

The use of stone on the building façade provided a sense of strength and permanence to the building's exterior. It also provided a physical connection to this region of the country. All of the stone on the barrier walls came from sites within the state of Oklahoma. The use of stone in the design of the Federal Campus brought with it a unique design challenge. In the aftermath of the Murrah bombing, the Federal Government rewrote its security and blast mitigation guidelines. In light of these revised guidelines, traditional hand-set stone might dislodge from the wall during an explosion. The concern was that the presence of cavities and voids between the stone and a back-up wall created a weak point in the system in the event of a blast.

A new stone-setting technique, eliminating the voids in the wall, had to be developed for this project. In order to minimize debris in the event of a blast, 27.58 MPa (4,000 psi) grout was required to secure the veneer stone to the concrete wall. The problem was how to achieve a monolithic pour. How could the contractor ensure that the high-strength grout would flow around the voids in the stone? Learning from several mock-ups, the solution was a new method for constructing a stone wall. The process involved attaching 3.8cm (1 ½ inch) thick furring strips to the face of a

Israeli Foreign Ministry,
Jerusalem, 2002. Exterior view
of onyx blast-resistent wall.

below Detail of stone connection back to metal framing
during construction.

page 29 below Israel Foreign
Ministry, façade section.
1 Perforated metal sunscreen
2 Steel sunscreen support
3 Catwalk
4 Hollow steel section skylight
5 Steel beam
6 Tapered concrete column
7 Wood screen
8 Sand blasted glass floor
9 Steel channel
10 Onyx panels
11 Stone floor
12 Elliptical steel columns
13 Glazing
14 Concrete floor

cast-in-place concrete wall, attaching a wire
mesh to those strips, and installing an outside
form 9cm (3.5 inches) away from the mesh.
Stones were then placed in the 9cm (3.5 inch)
void in 0.6m (2 foot) lifts. Grout was poured
into the system in two lifts. The grout filled
the voids between the concrete wall, the wire
mesh and the stone. Once all the lifts were
completed, the wall was sandblasted to reveal
the integral stone facing. A stone sealer was
applied to the finished wall to restore the color
and sheen of the local stone.

In seeking to protect building occupants, the
Oklahoma Federal Campus design addressed
four primary concerns: perimeter protection,
progressive collapse prevention, debris mitigation, and hardened internal partitions. Many
details of the building's design are not available to the public. The standoff distances from
unsecured areas are at least 15m (50 feet),
and the concrete walls and windows are
designed to resist blast loadings from those
distances. Cast-in-place concrete walls 30cm
(12 inches) thick form the building's perimeter
on the façades closest to the streets. The exterior walls are load-bearing and enable forces
to arch over any damaged portions. This alternative path approach provides for the redistri-
bution of loads resulting from the removal of
any single column. An important consideration in this type of enclosure is not only
strength but ductility.

Ductility

Stone and concrete can provide the strength
required for blast design. However, the goal for
many building designers is to prevent building
occupants from having to work in dark, ugly
concrete bunkers buried under the ground.
The Israeli Foreign Ministry, completed in
2002 in Jerusalem, was designed to meet
this challenge by the architectural firm of Diamond and Schmitt. Their solution provided
blast design with ductility. A ductile material is
capable of being stretched or deformed without fracturing. Ductility is an important char-
acteristic in blast design. Stone and concrete
are not ductile materials unless they are combined with metals like steel and aluminum.

The public building complex at the Israeli Foreign Ministry is configured to accommodate
elements appropriate to the State of Israel
and its ceremonial functions. In ceremonial
fashion there is an atrium and reception hall
for heads of state and dignitaries. This was a
structure that had to be both beautiful and
safe. The innovative design of the wall assembly for the reception building consists of a
structure that permits light penetration while
maintaining heightened security requirements.
The stone wall system has been designed
specifically to resist the horizontal thrust that
would result from an exterior bomb blast.
The central structure of the atrium consists of
12 concrete columns that support a skylight
roof above. A steel frame is bracketed off of
these columns to provide a secondary outer
structure. This second structure consists of
20 x 10cm (7 $^4/_5$ x 3 $^9/_{10}$ inch) elliptical steel
columns that support the barrier wall. This
barrier wall is enclosed by 30 horizontal aluminum channels, which carry 3cm (1 $^1/_4$ inch)
onyx panels.

Directly behind the stone panels are a series
of vertical airplane-gauge stainless steel
wires that are suspended from a flexible 5cm
(2 inch) diameter steel pipe. The wall system
has been designed to resist an exterior blast,
which would be absorbed by the stone and
secondary aluminum structure. Wooden
screens located along the walkways in the
atrium provide additional protection for occu-

Israel Foreign Ministry, interior view of onyx wall.

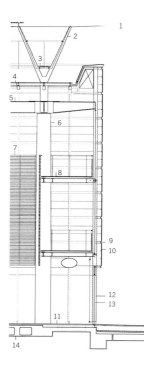

pants by catching smaller pieces of debris during an explosion. The screens also allow visitors to pass through the ceremonial space without disrupting events in the atrium area below. Although the wall would be destroyed in a large blast, the main structural elements and people inside the building would be protected. Testing of this system was necessary to verify the performance of this innovative enclosure system. A full-scale mock-up of the façade was constructed in the desert outside of Jerusalem. A controlled bomb blast pushed the mock-up stone inwards and onto the wire net, causing the cables to go into tension. The pipe on which the wires were strung collapsed further, absorbing energy from the explosion. Although the stone was fractured by the bomb blast, this was expected and the test was successful. It proved the ductile nature of the entire system. In this case, stone breakage due to impact is expected. However, in some projects it can be an unnecessary problem with some building enclosure systems.

Stone Breakage

Unlike blast design, traditional enclosure designs provide façades to resist uniformly distributed loads on a façade without breaking. Although a 1.44 kPa (30 psf) wind load can quickly add up to thousands of pounds in force over a large area, a much smaller 1.11 kN (250 pound) concentrated load can be the breaking point of a façade panel that has been cut too thin.

The Indiana Limestone Institute strongly recommends that Indiana Limestone be milled to dimensions not less than 5.08cm (2 inches). In contrast, the trend in Continental Europe has been to use considerably thinner limestone, usually between 3 and 4cm (1 1/4 – 1 1/2 inches). When using thin limestone cladding, considerable caution is required if thickness is to be reduced. Unlike many other commonly used cladding stones such as granite, limestone may suffer considerable weathering during the lifespan of the building. Given that limestone usually exhibits significantly lower

Section of Palace of Justice building.
1 Limestone base had a history of breakage due to small impact loads.

right The Palace of Justice, Bordeaux, 1999.

below The new Palace of Justice building, completed in 1999, was constructed with a stone base composed of panels that were cut too thin and broke easily under contact.

below right The original Palace of Justice building was constructed of large stone blocks that have weathered with time.

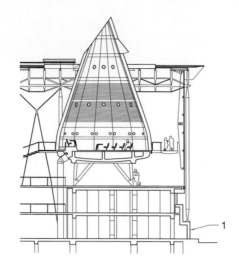

compressive and flexural strength than granite, on thin panels this weathering and consequent loss of strength may lead to rapid failure in service as the stone becomes unable to sustain imposed structural or wind loads. The loss of a few millimeters in thickness from a 10cm (3 $^9/_{10}$ inch) thick stone wall may be acceptable but in a 3cm (1 $^1/_4$ inch) thick veneer panel this may prove disastrous.

Completed in 1998, the new Palais de Justice building in Bordeaux provides seven unique courtrooms, administrative offices, and a large public space leading to the courtrooms. The seven courtrooms are pod-shaped, timber-clad volumes, supported by concrete pilotis. The wooden courtrooms combine high-tech geometry with traditional construction materials. Recent developments in computerized machinery were essential to the production of the complex curves and acoustic perforation of the internal maple-veneered finishes.

The base of the building consists of a limestone wall. Using the same stone as the original Palace of Justice building, the designers tried to make a connection between the two very different buildings. In an effort to match the stone of the old Palace of Justice, the new stone was sandblasted. This gave the stone a weathered appearance and texture similar to the original weathered building. However, the new stone cladding was made of thin stone panels and smaller stone blocks than were used with the old Palace of Justice. It is believed that the loss of thickness due to

sandblasting contributed to a design that could not resist the impact loads often found at the street level of a building. The stone at the base of the new building underwent regular breakage and had to be replaced with thicker stone.

Many times the thickness and finish of the stone are correctly designed. However, the impact loads imposed on it are too large, for example construction loads. In 2002, the MOMA in New York underwent a major addition. The historic sculptural garden was converted into a construction site with equipment and materials not considered in the original design of the paving system constructed in 1953. The stone paving has received considerable damage during the new construction process. Some of the large thick granite paving blocks have literally cracked in half. Thickness and finish are not the only factor in maintaining an architectural material's appearance. Edges are the most susceptible area of a stone, concrete or masonry wall.

The MOMA expansion in New York City brought large concentrated loads on the garden pavers. The result was broken paving blocks.

right Holocaust Memorial, Berlin, 2004.

right Section through the Memorial.
1 Seminar Room
2 Foyer
3 Room of Names
4 Room of Families

Edges

Sharp edges are often desired, but difficult to produce and maintain in concrete, stone and masonry. As designers strive for crisp corners to their building elements, they must consider how building materials will perform against the force of impact. Traditional corner details in concrete and stone often incorporate miters and eased edges to allow for some physical abuse by the end users. Other projects want sharp edges that challenge the end users' ability to maintain it.

The Holocaust Memorial, completed in December 2004 in Berlin, is designed with 2,711 gray precast concrete pillars with sharp corner edges. The field of pillars is composed of 0.91 x 2.44m (3 x 8 foot) pillars or stiles of varying heights ranging from approximately 0.46 to 4.57m (1 foot 6 inches to 15 feet). Consistently separated by a 0.91m (3 foot) wide path paved in small cubic blocks embedded in gravel, the pillars provide a rolling topography over the 20,235m² (5 acre) site. An underground Information Center with exhibition galleries, seminar room, a bookshop and offices is covered with a cast-in-place coffered ceiling that repeats the contours of the large precast blocks above. All of the concrete in the space was left unfinished to contribute to the exhibit's stark appearance.

The concrete stiles are composed of reinforced, self-compacting concrete that was prefabricated off-site. Each stile was reviewed against an approved prototype before it was shipped to the site and lowered into place with a crane. The color uniformity, finish, and corner details are greatly aided by the self-compacting concrete that fills all voids in a tightly fabricated precast concrete formwork. The sharp corners were for the most part intact after installation; however, they have suffered

minor defects with normal abrasion from construction and general use.

Typically sharp corners are hard to maintain with a brittle material like concrete. Traditional cast-in-place corners can be weaker because water leaks out of formwork corners, reducing the water available for full concrete hydration. Chamfered corners are typically used to improve seals and provide a less vulnerable edge to impact forces. Chamfered edges are made with triangular strips. They make strip-

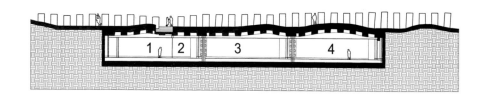

ping the form easier and prevent corners from leaking cement paste. The finished product is also less vulnerable to abrasion. Sharp corners are best achieved with watertight, precisely fabricated corners. If the joints are not tight and concrete mix water escapes from the form, color variation and material strength loss can occur. For this reason sharp corners are more susceptible to breakage. The corners at the Holocaust Memorial are in very good condition; however, chipped edges are fairly frequent.

One of the most difficult edges to maintain in architecture is a bench in a public plaza. Skateboarders have scarred our urban fabric with grind marks. Challenging the abilities of our youths, designers have developed a multitude of skateboard deterrent details to solve the problem. By using stepping curbs and

right In contrast to the Holocaust Memorial concrete blocks, beveled edges reduce the risk of chipping at a garden sculpture west of Munich.

below The 111 South Wacker office building, Chicago, has skateboard-proof walls which are stepped, non-continuous and curved in two dimensions.

benches, or applying metallic speed bumps to these surfaces, designers hope to prevent the impact of sport enthusiasts.

The 111 South Wacker office building in downtown Chicago, completed in 2005 by Goettsch Partners, combines a series of inconspicuous design features to deter skateboarders from marking the benches and

planters at the base of the building. On the north side of the building, separating the sidewalk from an ultratransparent cable wall system, a series of stepped curved stone benches have proven to be uninviting to the skateboard community. By curving the edges of the benches in both section and plan, skateboarders have found the site unusable and have moved on to other locations in the city.

The Lincoln Park Zoo, Regenstein Center for African Apes, designed by Goettsch Partners, has a sharp corner to the exterior gorilla habitat.

Because the corner is exposed to the gorillas and keepers at grade level, the durable corner was fabricated as a solid unit and beveled to resist chipping. Regenstein Center for African Apes, 2004, Chicago.

How Can Buildings Be Protected from Impact?

Stone, concrete and masonry are obviously very durable materials, able to resist impact loads; however, as the thickness of these materials is reduced with innovations in material fabrication, designers must understand that they become more vulnerable to impact failure. Architectural details must consider potential impacts at street level from luggage to skateboarders. Specific finishes and profiles are better able to take abuse. For example, a thermal (rough finish) on stone will hide abrasions better than a polished finish.

Blast design has become a factor in many new buildings, and stone, concrete or masonry is typically part of the solution. Structural considerations including redundancy, ductility, and debris mitigation can all be used to provide a system that resists progressive collapse. By providing steel embedded in concrete, contemporary projects combine ductility with fire resistance. Both of these are critical for the impact of an explosion. In many cases, the enclosure is sacrificial, providing permanent deformation in order to absorb the hazardous forces of an explosion. Life safety is the goal for this type of design solution. It is expected that damage will occur to the building elements. The concrete and stone elements will break. The goal of the system is safety and security of people and property near and inside the enclosure. From baseballs to bombs, concrete, stone and masonry enclosures can resist the forces thrown at them when designed for impact.

Lessons Learned

1
The Oklahoma City bombing proved to be a painful example of the importance for building structures to sustain significant local damage and remain standing.
2
Two major considerations in blast-resistant design: the loss of structural load-carrying capacity/stability and the fragmentation and propulsion of architectural and other building components, which become projectile threats to life safety.
3
The strength of an enclosure system ist not the only property to consider when designing to resist an explosion. Ductility of a wall system is critical to absorbing extreme forces.
4
Stone is a brittle material that has strength limitations when reduced in thickness. The finish applied to a material can alter its strength. A sandblast or bush-hammered finish to stone will reduce the flexural strength of the material. This can be critical when designing for localized loading from impact on thin stone material.
5
Successful plaza design must anticipate the misuse by skateboarders. A variety of techniques can be used in the design of benches and curbs to make them unappealing to this group.

Efflorescence

Architects have used masonry materials since the beginning of time. The Egyptians built monuments to their kings, the Greeks built temples for their gods, and the Romans constructed arenas for assembling large groups. Today, masonry remains a staple for buildings that are intended to last. Although construction techniques have evolved, common problems in masonry still exist. One problem that brick, concrete and stone have in common is

efflorescence. Efflorescence can be defined as the deposit of soluble compounds carried by water onto the surface of a building. Sometimes described as "new building bloom", the chalky powder is a common nuisance for many architects, buildings and building owners. The sporadic blemishes can tarnish the rich texture of façades in new construction. Efflorescence can disappear after a short period of time, as the new building dries out and rainwater rinses the façade clean of the salt deposits. However, if the source of the problem is not stopped, efflorescence can riddle a building for years. If left untreated, the consolidation of powdery salts can crystallize and become a serious detriment to a building envelope. If trapped behind the surface of a wall, the expansive properties of efflorescence can cause cracking, spalling, and lead to structural problems.

The causes of efflorescence can vary; however, the following factors must be present for it to surface on a building. First, there must be water movement through the wall to dissolve the salt compounds. This is a critical factor, and efflorescence can commonly be traced to water infiltration in buildings. Leaking walls or ineffective roof flashing transitions are a precursor to the marks of efflorescence. The

above New building bloom.

right The use of Portland cement to replace lime in mortar has been found to increase the amount of the efflorescence on our buildings.

page 35 Efflorescence can be a problem with modern buildings with brick façades. Auditorium Parco della Musica, Rome, 2002.

right Large amounts of efflorescence appear on the unprotected exterior walls. Covered walls show no sign of efflorescence. Auditorium Parco della Musica.

below Raked mortar joints provide poor weatherability as compared to concave or flush joints. Auditorium Parco della Musica.

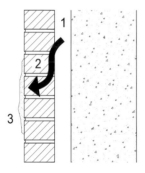

above Common factors of efflorescence
1 Water source
2 Water soluble components in wall
3 Evaporating water must reach the surface leaving salt deposits behind.

right Site plan of theater complex. Auditorium Parco della Musica.

second factor is that water soluble components must be in or adjacent to the wall system. The source of water soluble compounds can be the brick façade of a building, the concrete back-up system of a structure, the mortar used in a stone façade, or even the ground material at the base of an exterior wall. The final factor to the problem is that the water moving through the system must be able to reach an exterior surface of the wall. A new richly textured exterior wall can be riddled with white blotches that appear like pimples on a teenager's face. When the powdery material reaches the surfaces of a building to the dismay of the building owner, everyone scrambles for a solution to this age-old problem.

Efflorescence can be found in concrete and stone enclosures; however, it is most common in brick façades. Efflorescence is for the most part a visual defect and it rarely causes structural problems. There are many products available to treat the issue. Many believe efflorescence is to be expected to a small degree for brick buildings and suggest it will eventually go away once the salt deposits are depleted. What is critical to understand is that if the source of water movement is not stopped and soluble materials are still present, efflorescence will frustrate building owners for years. Most efflorescence is noticed on the exterior of a masonry wall, but more damaging efflo-

rescence can occur below the wall surface. It is amazing that a construction defect that dates back to Roman times still riddles contemporary architecture today.

The Auditorium Parco della Musica in Rome was designed to serve as a multifunction complex dedicated to music. Constructed over the remains of a Roman villa dating to the 4th century, the site consists of three concert halls and one large amphitheater. The scale of these "music box" structures is enormous. Each of the building elements resembles a large beetle resting on a masonry plinth surrounded by luxurious vegetation. The goal of these brick and metal enclosures was to acoustically separate each of the concert halls. All three of the buildings share similar details. The roofs are composed of metal-standing seam roofing, covering a wood structure, with a concrete foundation surrounded

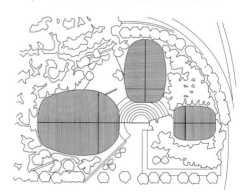

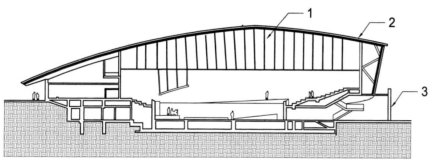

above Large wood-framed structure wrapped in metal rests on masonry walls. Auditorium Parco della Musica.

below Building section of music hall. Auditorium Parco della Musica.
1 Laminated wood structure
2 Metal standing seam roofing
3 Roman brick base

by a base of Roman brick masonry walls. Each of the masonry walls is capped with a travertine stone coping. Although the Auditorium Parco della Musica was completed in 2002, the effects of efflorescence are still visible on many of the building's exterior masonry walls in 2005.

The origin of the water soluble components is most likely in the Roman brick and mortar. The source of moving water could be attributed to the travertine coping at the top of the walls. Unsealed travertine has a high absorption rating. This porous horizontal surface at the top of a wall can wick water down into the cavity below. In addition to the absorptive

properties of the travertine cap material, the stone coping mortar joints on a regular interval allow for a second path for water to penetrate the top horizontal surface. On the face of the wall the masonry joints have been raked back for aesthetic reasons. Although this helps create a richer wall texture, the raked joints provide an easy path for water to infiltrate the wall. The ability of water to move through the wall is facilitated by the lack of flashing below the coping and the absence of effective weep holes at the base of the wall. Thus penetrating water can be trapped in the wall cavity and will evaporate through the body of the brick and mortar joints to the exterior. This moving water carries soluble components and eventually evaporates on the face of the building, leaving patches of white powder in its wake. It should be noted that the masonry exterior walls of the building that are protected from rainwater by large overhangs do not show signs of efflorescence. In order to better understand efflorescence and the potentially serious nature of the defect, one needs to examine the chemical composition of the problem.

Chemical Composition

Efflorescence is a calcium or alkaline salt which forms as a blotchy, powdery or crystalline deposit on the surface of masonry walls and concrete products. There are many kinds of salt that can be detected in samples of efflorescence. The following are a list of the most common:

Sodium sulfate
Sodium carbonate
Sodium bicarbonate
Sodium silicate
Potassium sulfate
Calcium sulfate
Calcium carbonate
Magnesium sulfate

Testing of brick for efflorescence.

38 39

Crystallized efflorescence in a masonry wall.

If the efflorescence contains sodium sulfate it can lead to a problem called "salt hydration distress" (SHD) which means that the sodium sulfate combines with water, causing the mineral to expand and take up more space. Depending on the temperature and humidity at the building location, sodium sulfate can change between the anhydrous (without water) and hydrous (with water) states. As the salt converts back and forth between states, the forces created by the volume change can spall the adjacent brick, concrete or stucco material. SHD is also more prevalent when relative humidity fluctuates during the course of a day, such as in coastal regions of California and Australia.

The more common examples of efflorescence take two basic forms. The first is the powdery surface spread uniformly over a wall which can give a pigmented concrete block or clay brick a faded appearance. This efflorescence is easily treated with a light application of products designed to remove the salts from the surface of the wall. The second form is a crystallized material that is more difficult to remove.

Crystallization

If left untreated the powdery efflorescence that can blemish a wall will continue through many cycles of depositing salts to the surface, re-dissolving when new water occurs, drying out afterwards. Finally the deposits can form crystals on the wall which become tightly bonded to the surface material. Crystallized efflorescence is more difficult to remove than the powdery type and can lead to serious structural damage to brick and mortar cavity walls.

Brick and Mortar Joints

The occurrence and amount of efflorescence often has some relationship to the composition of the mortar used in a wall assembly. For example, a particular type of brick and a certain type of mortar could have no occurrence of efflorescence; however, the same brick with another mortar may produce a wall that has extensive salt deposits. The large quantities of sodium and potassium salts (usually sulfates) in most efflorescence suggest Portland cement as their source. The use of Portland cement to replace lime in mortar has been found to increase the amount of efflorescence on our buildings. Efflorescence can be minimized by reducing the amount of Portland cement, sodium and potassium salts present in the mortar batch.

Although mortar is a governing source of the salts found in efflorescence, it is not the only source. Bricks may contain appreciable amounts of salts which are dissolved by moisture and brought to the surface through time. Bricks can be tested to determine the amount of salts present. The test consists of placing a brick on end in a pan of distilled water for seven days. With time the water is drawn upwards through the brick and evaporates on the surface of the brick. If soluble salts are present in the brick, they will be deposited on its surface.

The absorption rate of a brick also influences the amount of efflorescence that will develop on the wall. A brick with a high rate of water absorption combined with a high cement mor-

Exposed concrete wall shows evidence of slight efflorescence. Expansion of University of Cincinnati School of Architecture and Interior Design.

right Small whites streaks on concrete wall could be the result of efflorescence or latex additive in the concrete. Our Lady of the Angels, Los Angeles, 2002.

tar will produce large deposits of efflorescence. The same mortar used with a brick having a moderate rate of absorption will produce only small amounts of efflorescence. By using a brick with a low rate of absorption with the same mortar, the masonry wall can be virtually unmarked by efflorescence. In materials that allow free movement of water, efflorescence can prove to be a problem. By restricting the amount of water movement through a wall, efflorescence can be minimized.

Concrete

Most people think of efflorescence as a problem for brick buildings. However, because Portland cement is one of the contributing factors to the issue, concrete walls can also fall prey to the chalky white deposits. A concrete mix typically has several ingredients including sand, aggregate, and Portland cement. Cements are typically the greatest source of soluble materials contributing to efflorescence. Concrete walls exposed to wetting are susceptible to efflorescence. Because the

natural color of concrete is very close to the white powdery residue of efflorescence, it is less noticeable and tolerated more frequently.

The University of Cincinnati School of Architecture and Interior Design expansion contains exterior concrete walls that are exposed to rain on all sides. These walls exhibit a mild film of efflorescence on the exterior surface noticeable as a white powder substance. However, because the concrete substrate resembles the color and texture of efflorescence, it is not perceived as a problem.

right Small windows prevent inmates from escaping. Metropolitan Correctional Center, Chicago, 1975.

below Dripping water from an air-conditioning unit is the cause of efflorescence on this masonry wall.

right Spalled concrete at window detail. Metropolitan Correctional Center.

page 41 Exterior cast in place concrete walls. Metropolitan Correctional Center.

The Metropolitan Correctional Center in Chicago was constructed with sleek concrete walls and narrow windows to prevent the escape of inmates. The building is nested in the heart of Chicago's downtown business district. Although the walls may prevent the escape of inmates, the passage of water has not been stopped in all areas of the exterior wall. Spalling concrete can be seen as a side effect of moving water and of salt deposits. The white efflorescence film shown near an exterior window provides the smoking gun to a problem of water migration through the wall.

Efflorescence can commonly occur in brickwork adjoining concrete material. In this situation concrete is frequently wetted from rain and snow melting on it. The soluble salts of the concrete are dissolved and can be carried into the brickwork beneath. Salts which cause efflorescence may originate in the concrete masonry back-up behind the brick facing of a wall. Initially, the outer face of the wall may be free of salt deposits. However, with prolonged dampness of the interior wall, salts can be carried into the brickwork, leading to efflorescence on the surface. For this reason, masonry walls near defective drains or roof flashings are often marked by efflorescence, while other parts of the building appear to be unaffected by the problem. Similarly, walls that are splashed by water from sprinklers, mechanical equipment, or fountains can be prone to marks of efflorescence.

Acrylic and latex additives are sometimes used as admixtures to concrete masonry and mortar. These white products will sometimes leach out to the surface and appear like efflorescence. Although similar in appearance, the removal process is different. Efflorescence is not limited to brick and concrete façades. Because efflorescence is related to mortar, it can be a problem with stone façades, where walls are tied together with mortar joints.

page 42 Undulating Kasota dolomitic limestone walls resemble cliffs carved out by nature.
National Museum of the American Indian, Washington, D.C., 2004.

right Large overhang protects the front entrance to the museum.
National Museum of the American Indian.

Stone

Located in front of the United States Capitol, the National Museum of the American Indian was added to the National Mall in 2004. It was the last available site on the Mall, just south of the East Building of the National Gallery of Art. In strong contrast to its classic Greek and Roman architectural neighbors, the museum resembles a rock formation carved out of a sandstone canyon by wind and water. The building is clad in more than 2,400 tons of Kasota dolomitic limestone and required approximately 50,000 pieces of cut stone of varying sizes. The five-story-tall museum has a cantilevered overhang at the main east entrance, sheltering visitors from the sun and rain. The base of the building, surrounded by pools and fountains, has a band of American-mist granite. It is at this location that traces of efflorescence can be seen in the limestone wall where a fountain splashes water onto the base of the building. Splashing water from the fountain penetrates the porous limestone wall at these locations. As the water evaporates from the cool north face of the building, salt deposits are left on the surface of the stone.

The undulating walls of the Museum required extensive flashing details and transitions. It is at these locations where water has the potential to infiltrate the wall. Marks of efflorescence can be seen below a northern roof transition. It should be noted that all of the efflorescence markings visible on the wall were on the north side of the building. Because of the newness of the building, some of these marks could be attributed to "new building bloom."

New Building Bloom

Efflorescence has often been characterized as "new building bloom" because it commonly occurs shortly after a new wall is constructed. The reason for this is that during the construction of an exterior wall the system is often left unprotected. During this period, incomplete cavity walls and materials may experience penetration by a large amount of water behind the outer face of the wall from rain. After the final coping has been installed at the top of the wall, the excess water from the construction period will work its way out of the building skin toward the exterior. As the excess water travels through the wall, it brings the soluble construction material with it, leaving the salt deposits in its wake. Once this water has left the wall, the efflorescence should not reappear because the source of the water was solely due to the construction process. New building bloom can be minimized by covering the cavity wall during construction in order to prevent the penetration of rainwater or snow. If efflorescence appears on a wall that has been property-protected during the assembly of the wall, it can be a signal that wall leaks are the problem. If a wall is well protected during construction, efflorescence need not occur.

left Efflorescence marks near the water feature.
National Museum of the American Indian.

right Efflorescence marks at roof transition.
National Museum of the American Indian.

Coping and Flashing Conditions

Efflorescence is initiated by the flow of water through building materials. If the flow of water is excessive and uncontrolled, unsightly blotches on building elements can result. Effective copings at the top of masonry walls and parapets are critical to preventing water infiltration problems. The Vontz Center for Molecular Studies in Cincinnati, Ohio, has isolated areas where the white powder of efflorescence suggests the infiltration of water. Signage at the entrance to the building depicts an example of a coping condition that struggles to keep water out of the wall system. Capped with a Rowlock course of brick, the top of the sign wall has unprotected horizontal masonry joints at approximately 100mm (4 inches) on center. These mortar joints allow water into the wall cavity. Infiltrating water finds its way back to the surface of the wall, carrying salt deposits with it. The deposits are left behind as a reminder that masonry joints on a horizontal surface should be expected to crack and let in water. A possible solution to the water problem is to cap the top course of the wall with a metal coping. Although slightly different in appearance, the coping would shed water away from the signage and protect the wall from water infiltration. Other areas of the building show signs of ineffective flashing details that have left streaks of white efflorescence. Penetrating rainwater is the source of most of the damage; however, water can also come from the surrounding earth if masonry is not separated from soil.

Wicking from Soil

The movement of water from the base of a foundation can lead to efflorescence. Soils containing soluble salts can be wicked up through a masonry wall leaving powdery white deposits on the surface of the building skin. In order to prevent this problem from occurring, masonry walls should not come in contact with soils. Soils can typically contain a fair amount of salts and organic materials. During the design phase of a building, it is important to separate masonry products from the surrounding soil. Improper storage of material on the ground prior to using in construction is also a common cause of salt contamination. One of the most difficult conditions to rectify on a building is water that comes from soils in contact with masonry at the base of a building. At locations where soils do come in contact with masonry, waterproofing coatings are required to prevent the transfer of water and staining salts from contacting porous wall surfaces. At planter locations where water is not contained or properly weeped through planter drains, staining from organic materials can form on the face of a wall. These stains are a signal that water is not traveling in the intended path and that repair of the waterproofing will be required. The Canadian Embassy in

1

2

Building sign at Vontz Center for Molecular Studies at the University of Cincinnati, Ohio, 1999.
1 Existing brick coping allows water to infiltrate the wall
2 A solution to the water problem would be to install a metal coping

right Ineffective flashings can result in efflorescent stains. Vontz Center for Molecular Studies.

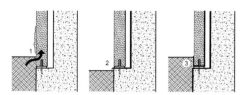

Masonry must be separated from soil material.

1 Limestone in contact with soils can lead to efflorescence and staining of the wall.

2 Base flashing under elevated limestone material can help prevent wicking of water from soil.

3 Where limestone is located below grade, dampproofing must be installed to protect the stone.

A brick cap above the building sign allows water to infiltrate the wall.
Vontz Center for Molecular Studies.

right Masonry building signage at the entrance to the building.
Vontz Center for Molecular Studies.

Washington, D.C., has a series of balconies at the interior courtyard which show signs of migrating water. The green stains that mark the outside face of these walls are a signal that moisture from the soil is evaporating through the wall. Constant moisture present on building materials can provide conditions of growing algae and mold.

A base flashing, installed above grade between foundation and masonry wall, will prevent upward movement of ground water which otherwise might carry salts into the wall. If the cause of the efflorescence is due to rising water table or ground water, the solution does not come easily. It is critical to design adjacent horizontal surfaces to drain away from masonry walls and to provide dampproof course at the level where the water table is anticipated.

Green stains indicate moisture from the planters.
Canadian Embassy, Washington, D.C., 1989.

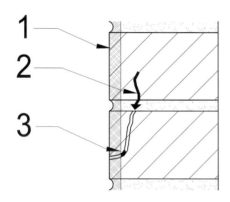

Some water repellants can cause more harm than good.
1 Silicone sealers penetrate the face of the wall.
2 Water penetrates wall through defects, evaporates out as vapor, but leaves salts at line of sealer.
3 Crystallization of salts can cause spalling of surface material from internal pressures.

right Efflorescence can scar the face of a building.

Cold Weather Friend

Efflorescence is common in the winter months in northern climates because lower temperatures slow down the evaporation process of water. For this reason, it is more prevalent on north-facing walls than south-facing walls. As evaporation is slowed down, salt deposits do not evaporate with the water and are left behind on the surface of the wall. In the summer months, the rate of evaporation of moisture from a masonry wall can be very high. This allows for moisture to quickly move through the wall to the outer surface, allowing for less of the salt deposits to be left in its path. In contrast, the winter months provide the perfect environment for the slow evaporation of water from a wall and thus the accumulation of efflorescence. Efflorescence can be brought on by climatic and environmental changes. In late fall, winter, and early spring efflorescence can appear after a rainy period, when evaporation is much slower and temperatures are cooler.

How Can Efflorescence Be Removed?

Efflorescence can be removed much more easily than other types of stains on a wall. Typically, the efflorescence salt deposits are water soluble and if present on an exterior surface may disappear with normal wetting of the surface by rain. Powdery efflorescence can be removed with a dry brush or water and a stiff brush. Light detergents can be used to clean the wall of other stains during the process. During the removal process, it is important not to saturate the wall as this will push the salts into the surface. The objective is to remove the salt deposits in order to prevent their reoccurrence.

The exterior of a brick façade is typically "washed down" soon after completion. This process cleans the wall of excess mortar and construction stains. While acids are frequently used to remove efflorescence, they can contain chlorides which contribute to efflorescence. This is one reason why many buildings show signs of efflorescence shortly after an acid washdown of a masonry wall. Another

reason is that the water used for rinsing the wall has gone into the masonry and brought out more of the salts.

Heavy accumulation of efflorescence, in the crystallized form, can usually be removed with a solution of muriatic or nitric acid and scrubbing (1 part acid to 12 parts water). Caution should be taken with the application of acid because of its hazardous nature. The wall must be saturated with water both before and after scrubbing. In addition to harming the applicator, muriatic acid can rust metal surfaces.

Less common efflorescence salts that change their chemical structure during their formation will require proprietary compounds to be removed. For these severe cases, chemical products are available to take care of the problem. These products are specially designed for efflorescence removal and do not contain chlorides that contribute to the problem.

How Can Efflorescence Be Avoided?

Since so many factors may contribute to the development of efflorescence, no one precautionary measure can be expected to take care of all potential conditions. The goal is to reduce all of the contributing factors to a minimum. Each condition must be explored separately, the first being the materials that compose the wall. In order for efflorescence to form, soluble salts must be present. Some control may therefore be taken by the selection of materials which are low in salt content. Clay bricks, for example, may be tested to determine whether they contain salts which will contribute to efflorescence. The use of lime and of low-alkali Portland cement and low-alkali masonry cement will greatly reduce the capacity of mortar to contribute to efflorescence. Hydrated limes are relatively pure and can have four to 10 times less efflorescing potential than cements. Careful storage of the materials on the job site is also necessary to avoid contamination from salt-carrying ground water.

Water is the vehicle used for the salt deposits. Stopping the path of water will stop efflorescence. Failure to repair cracked or broken mortar joints can contribute to the problem. When efflorescence is linked to abnormal wetting of the wall, as from a roof leak or sprinkler head, it is critical to correct these problems prior to removing the efflorescence. In a similar manner, when the cause of efflorescence is water penetration of a coping, the solution is installing a damp-proof course or metal coping to interrupt the movement of water into the brickwork.

Water repellents used to suppress efflorescence are available in the construction market. In order for water repellents to work effectively, water must be able to evaporate through them. However, the salt molecules which are larger in size are prevented from escaping by the coating. Penetrating sealers are designed to create a barrier that stops salt migration, yet breathes out water vapor. Silicone water repellents may appear to control efflorescence by stopping water intrusion; however, they can cause greater damage if they prevent the escape of crystallized efflorescing salts, thus forcing the building material to absorb the expansive pressure of internal crystallization.

It can be hazardous to apply seals to walls that contain both moisture and salts. The moisture may evaporate through the treated surface, but salt deposits can accumulate behind the sealer near the surface. Localized accumulation of salts and their crystallization may cause the surface of the material to spall or flake off. The use of a silicone treatment to suppress efflorescence may be dangerous in cases where excessive water migration produces hydrostatic pressure buildup from entrapped salts below the surface. This is particularly true when there are large amounts of salts in the masonry and the units are soft and porous.

Lessons Learned

1
Efflorescence will continue to reappear as long as there is a source of soluble compounds present and water continues to move through the wall. Stopping the source of water is imperative to stopping the reappearance of efflorescence.

2
The potential for efflorescence can be minimized by choosing bricks rated non-efflorescing and by using low-alkali cement. Mortars with high lime/cement ratio also help reduce the risk of efflorescence.

3
Copings and parapets are especially susceptible to water infiltration. Stopping water intrusion at these locations will aid in stopping efflorescence at the masonry wall below.

4
Do not put masonry products in contact with soil. If masonry is in contact with soil it can wick up salts that can lead to staining and efflorescence. Elevated base flashing prevents the migration of water up a building wall.

5
It is important to cover the masonry wall cavity and materials during construction in order to minimize the amount of water inside the cavity. Incidental water inside the wall will eventually evaporate out of the wall; unfortunately, it may leave salt deposit behind. Reducing water movement after the completion of construction through proper design and detailing will minimize the risk of efflorescence.

6
Some surfaces are more prone to efflorescence because they are more permeable and promote water travel. Many bricks have higher soluble salts in some batches. The risk of efflorescence can be reduced if these two factors are considered when selecting building materials; however, because these building materials come from the earth, the potential for some water soluble salts will always be present.

teeth. Filling the fissures and cracks with resin material can make the stone look uniform and presentable. This type of repair has its own limitations and cannot mask all flaws in stone. Stone inclusions are embedded foreign material that can break up the uniform color and texture of a stone panel. Some stones, like marble, have veining and grain that can distract from the appearance of a façade if not properly matched. A single incorrectly oriented panel can look seriously out of place on a stone façade.

Man-made materials like concrete are more prone to irregularities of finish. Cast-in-place concrete has a history of being hidden from view. New trends in contemporary design have put concrete workmanship back in the spotlight. These designs are supported by new technologies such as self-compacting and ultrahigh strength concrete. However, even with these advances, concrete is a very unforgiving material with a long memory. Any mistakes in the pour will be cast in stone for all to remember. Heightened quality control measures are required when concrete is to be left exposed. Special techniques have been developed to minimize honeycombing, spalling and other surface irregularities. In order to gage these improvements, it is helpful to review an older architectural icon constructed of cast-in-place concrete.

Surface Defects

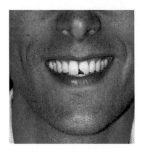

above Like a chipped tooth, surface defects on a façade can distract from an otherwise perfect smile.

right Broken stone panel at One South La Salle Street, Chicago.

page 49 The Jay Pritzker Pavilion at Millenium Park in Chicago, 2004. Cracks in concrete are virtually unavoidable. A shrinkage crack has tauntingly formed adjacent to the control joint designed to prevent it.

Surface defects can be a glaring distraction to the design of a building, just as a chipped tooth can distract from an otherwise perfect smile. Since the building's exterior often displays an image of the owner to the world, the builder should have sufficient knowledge of potential surface defects to prevent their occurrence.

Stone is a natural material, having inherent flaws and variations. The stone fabricator can make repairs to the appearance of a stone panel much as a dentist can repair cavities in

above left The poured-in-place concrete walls at the Salk Institute were to show how the building was constructed.

right above Honeycombing of concrete corners is not uncommon at the Salk Institute.

right below Bugholes are abundant on many of the walls at the Salk Institute.

The Salk Institute for Biological Studies in La Jolla, California, designed by architect Louis Kahn, was completed in 1965. This complex was designed in collaboration with the Institute's founder, Jonas Salk, M.D. Dr. Salk was the developer of the polio vaccine, and the Institute was designed to provide a home for future medical studies. The complex consists of two mirror-image structures that flank a grand courtyard, opening onto landscape to the east and the Pacific Ocean to the west. Each of the six-story buildings houses offices and laboratories. The careful selection of wood, stone, and concrete material was

aimed at making a maintenance-free building enclosure. The window units are framed in teak wood. The plaza provides a durable "façade to the sky" using travertine marble. The sharp edges of the stone gutters, which direct water to the famous axial water trough, have kept their crisp-sharp edges through the years. The most distinctive material in the complex is the concrete.

The cast-in-place concrete walls at the Salk Institute were created with a special mix designed to create a pinkish "pozzolanic" glow. Formwork boards went from floor to floor

In the 1990s, the Salk Institute was cramped for space and embarked on a controversial expansion to its campus. Many groups resisted adding to the site of such an architecturally significant work; but the east buildings completed in 1995 with the understanding that the finished details of the new buildings would match those of the original. In fact, a noticeable improvement in the surface details of the new buildings can be seen. The finish quality and uniformity of color on the new buildings is in strong contrast to the existing structure. Wall ties are perfectly executed and the form lines are flawless. The surface of the new walls is smooth with no large voids or irregularities. The outside corners are crisp with no spalling, chips or cracks. The new and old buildings at the Salk Institute serve as an excellent case study of how the concrete industry has improved finishing techniques over the past 40 years. In order to understand these improvements, it is important to analyze typical surface defects in concrete.

above The travertine paved plaza provides a beautiful "façade to the sky."

right The concrete finish of the new buildings at the Salk Institute have crisp corners and smooth surfaces free of any honeycombing or large bugholes.

Surface Defects in Cast-in-Place Concrete

Because concrete is made of a variety of materials, incorrect mixing or placing can lead to visual surface imperfections. These are not only unsightly; they can seriously reduce the concrete durability with consequential financial implications. Surface defects in cast-in-place concrete can take many forms. The following are the classic flaws that can arise with cast-in-place concrete.

Honeycombing

Honeycombing is a defect resulting in zones of concrete that are devoid of cement mortar. While these are generally visible at the surface, they can extend to some depth within the concrete. This flaw comes from a failure of the cement mortar to effectively fill the spaces between coarse aggregate particles. Its cause is typically linked to an inappropriate concrete composition or to inadequate compaction during a pour. The composition of the mix must be well graded and take into account the water content of sand and aggregate. The steel reinforcement must be detailed so as to allow the concrete mix to flow around the reinforcing bars, and between the bars and the formwork. Hence, concrete cover influences

with projecting joint marks between forms and exposed wall ties. Each of these elements provides a regular pattern on the walls. In the architect's words, "these joints are the beginning of ornament." Louis Kahn wanted to show in every way exactly how the concrete building was constructed. The goal at the time was not to make perfect concrete. The discoloration between pours is visible, wall ties were left exposed with chips and irregularities, and defects like honeycombing were left untouched. Once the concrete was set, there was no further processing of the finish, neither grinding, filling, nor painting.

Surface defects in cast-in-place concrete from form joints.
1 Offset
2 Fin

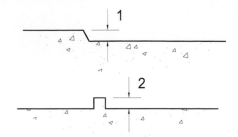

below Small crack in travertine paving, Salk Institute.

the size of aggregate in the concrete; the concrete mix must be able to flow into the reinforcement cover zone. Honeycombing can also result from formwork that is too flexible or poorly fixed; gaps in the formwork allow the cement grout to leak out.

Form Scabbing

Form scabs are surface defects caused by the movement of forms prior to the concrete setting. The most common defect comes from concrete sticking to the forms during stripping. This typically results when the forms are stripped too early and results in large voids in the finished wall. Another example of form scabbing can be seen in leakage of mortar onto the surface concrete of a lower lift because of movement of the formwork above.

Bugholes

Bugholes, also known as blowholes, are the result of entrapped air bubbles in the surface of hardened concrete. Bugholes often occur in vertical cast-in-place concrete surfaces and should not be considered a defect unless they are unusually large, 19mm ($^3/_4$ inch) or larger in diameter. Bugholes are principally caused by improper, often excessive, vibration. This problem can be worsened by the use of unsuitable concrete mixes; an overly stiff mix can cause increased bughole formation. Another cause can be impermeable formwork; this can prevent the passage of air bubbles across the concrete to formwork interface. Some formwork release agents, improperly applied, can contribute to this problem.

Aggregate Transparency

Dark areas reveal the locations of coarse aggregate particles near the surface. When the aggregate is not uniformly distributed, the pattern also will not be uniform. Several causes have been identified: flexible forms, causing a pumping action during compaction, incorrect mix design, and excessive vibration contribute to aggregate transparency.

Fins and Offsets

Cast-in-place concrete forms have size limitations and therefore require joints between units. If these joints are not sealed properly, a surface defect can result. Fins are narrow linear projections on a formed concrete surface, resulting from mortar flowing into the space between the forms. An offset is a step in the concrete surface due to an abrupt change in alignment of adjacent forms. It can occur either horizontally or vertically. Similar to a fin, an offset interrupts the smooth appearance of a surface. For smooth-formed concrete surfaces the maximum allowable offset or fin would be 3mm ($^1/_8$ inch).

above The concrete finish of the new buildings at the Salk Institute have crisp corners and smooth surfaces.

below left Finish, form lines, and tie holes on the Salk Institute expansion are virtually flawless.

below right Finish, form lines, and tie holes on the original Salk Institute were never intended to be perfect.

The Jay Pritzker Pavilion, Chicago, 2004, provides concrete control joints at ten feet on center in order to provide a uniform cracking of the concrete retaining walls. In some locations the cracks appear adjacent to the control joints.

Retaining walls display layer marks in the concrete. The Jay Pritzker Pavilion.

Cracks

Concrete cracks occur for a number of reasons, including shrinkage, thermal contraction, and subgrade settlement. As concrete cures, water evaporates and the material shrinks ever so slightly. Normal concrete can resist compression; however, it is weak in resisting tensile forces. If the shrinkage forces are greater than the concrete's developing tensile strength, early-age plastic shrinkage cracks will occur. This form of cracking principally results from an excessive rate of evaporation during the all-important curing period. It can be avoided by keeping the concrete surface damp during the curing process. Some shrinkage and thermal cracking forces will inevitably arise and are typically controlled by the provision of joints to define the crack location. Where cracking is particularly undesirable (as in the case of water-retaining structures), additional secondary reinforcement can be added to limit the crack width. Good practice enables us to control cracking.

Curling of Concrete Slabs

Concrete slabs on grade can curl up at joints and around the perimeter of the slab. In topping slab conditions the top slab can lose contact with the subbase material, curling up at the ends. Curling is most noticeable at construction control joints, but it can also occur at cracks and saw-cut joints. The cause of curling is differential shrinkage that occurs in a slab as the exposed top surface shrinks and

Cracks in the floor slab around an interior column oppose the anticipated crack direction. Cracking can be caused by improper isolation-joint design that does not provide relief at reentrant corners.

right Spalling at corroded reinforcement. Salk Institute.

far right Scaling of concrete slab exposed to cold weather.

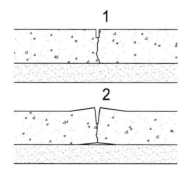

Curling at a saw-cut joint in slab.
1 Saw-cut joint prior to curling of concrete
2 Saw-cut joint after curling of concrete

the core does not. Although it is possible to repair curling in most slabs, prevention by controlling shrinkage is preferred. Good mix proportioning, proper curing, and placement of saw-cut joints can help to reduce the effects of curling.

Layer Marks

Prominent layer marks can occur as a result of inadequate compaction and long-time intervals between placing the layers. Layer marks can also result from a change in the composition of the concrete mix.

Scaling

Scaling of concrete can occur when water is absorbed into the concrete materials and freezes with low temperatures. This is particularly true of flatwork exposed to weather in cold climates. Scaling is often caused by the expansion and contraction of surface concrete due to the freeze/thaw cycling. This type of defect will typically appear near joints after a year of thermal cycling. The solution to this problem is to provide additional air entrainment to the mix, prior to pouring the concrete. Thin scaling can be caused by improper finishing and curing operations and is exacerbated by the application of snow and ice removal products such as salt.

Spalling and Reinforcement Marks

Spalling occurs as a result of environmental attack where the concrete cover to reinforcement is inadequate; the steel reinforcement close to the surface of the concrete rusts.

Rusting of the steel causes the volume of the steel to expand and break the surface of the concrete (See the chapter "Corrosion" for a more detailed explanation). As with scaling, spalling can also be caused by improper finishing and curing operations and is exacerbated by the application of snow and ice removal products such as salt.

Reinforcement marks arise when the concrete cover is absent, usually due to displacement of the reinforcement cage before or during the concreting operation. The bars soon rust and cause staining of the concrete surface.

Irregular Tie Holes

Tie bars connect in the gang form frames and prevent the forms from bulging out under the hydrostatic pressure of the liquid concrete. Tie holes are the void in a concrete surface left when a tie end is snapped off, broken back, or removed. Ties that are broken back or snapped off frequently leave irregular holes, whereas threaded internal disconnecting ties leave more uniform holes. Where spreader cones are used on the ties, the holes are uniform. Tie holes are normally filled; however, in exposed locations where they are spaced in a regular pattern, they have become an important architectural detail in contemporary design. Tie bar spacing must consider the strength of the panels. If the spacing between tie bars becomes too great, the formwork will bow out and create an uneven finished surface.

Cathedral of Our Lady of the Angels, Los Angeles, 2002.

below Tie holes in cast-in-place concrete can be covered with a variety of techniques.
1 Welded water stop plate
2 Metal or plastic cone
3 Wall thickness
4 Formwork anchor (threaded rod)
5 Plastic cone
6 Formwork
7 Filled with mortar
8 Plugged (e.g. with lead)
9 Filled and shaped with mortar
10 Filled with mortar

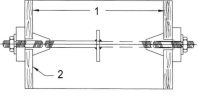

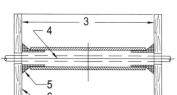

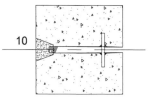

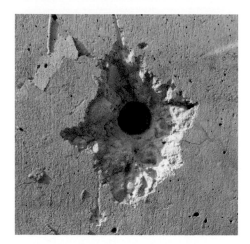

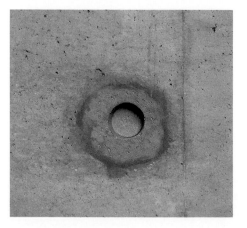

right Colored concrete poses a challenge to repair as seen by tie hole fix at Our Lady of the Angels.

The Forming of Concrete

Surface defects in concrete can be linked to the method of casting the material. Through the years, the techniques of forming concrete have improved, requiring architects to rethink how they use concrete. New products have provided designers with alternative methods of molding concrete in exciting new ways that reduce the risk of surface defects.

Cast-in-place Concrete

Completed in 125 A.D., the Pantheon provides one of the oldest surviving buildings constructed with cast-in-place concrete. Remarkable for its size, the dome was the largest built in ancient times. Without the use of steel reinforcement, the dome spans 43m (142 feet) in diameter and rises to a height of 22m (71 feet) above its base. Romans developed mortar for their concrete from fine volcanic ash (known as pozzolana), lime (from burnt limestone), and water. Added to this was crushed brick and animal blood. The builders of the Pantheon were very conscious of their materials and reduced the weight of the concrete from the base (heaviest) to the top of the dome (lightest) by using aggregate of different weights, the lightest aggregate used being pumice. After nearly 2000 years, we are continuing to refine the process of forming concrete.

right Spalling concrete is still visible on cast-in-place concrete walls of Wright's 1905 Unity Temple even after significant repairs to the structure in 2000.

right The Pantheon is one of the oldest surviving buildings constructed with cast-in-place concrete.

Formwork

Today, concrete formwork can be classified into two groups: absorbent and non-absorbent. Non-absorbent formwork is generally one of three different types: wood modified with synthetic resin, coated steel, or plastic formwork. Absorbent formwork draws water out of the surface of concrete by suction during the hardening process. Timber formwork is an example of absorbent formwork, which can leave surface defects from organic material in the wood, like wood sugar. By applying a pretreatment of cement wash followed by brushing, these defects can be avoided. The cement wash can also remove fine splinters from rough formwork. If not removed, the splinter can be left behind in the exposed concrete and give the concrete a yellowish appearance after the forms are removed. Absorbent formwork must be watered within 12 hours before pouring so that the formwork does not remove too much water from the curing concrete; water absorption will reduce the water/cement ratio at the surface of the concrete. This reduction can result in incomplete hydration of cement and seriously compromise the protective properties of the concrete cover to reinforcement. Color differences can occur due to formwork that sucks more or less water from the mix. Leakage of water from joints of forms draws cement and other fine particles toward joints and causes a slightly darker hydration discoloration.

The swelling of the wood, prior to pouring, helps make the formwork joints water tight. Fins are created when cement paste oozes out between the forms. Form joint construction can reduce the likelihood of fins in locations where concrete walls are to be left exposed. Too much swelling can cause the forms to warp and lift.

Smooth-form concrete used in exposed locations is obtained from smooth form-facing material arranged in an orderly and symmetrical manner with a minimum of seams. Tie holes and defects are patched, and fins and other projections larger than 3mm (1/8 inch) are removed. Small bugholes are acceptable; however, bugholes larger than 19mm (3/4 inch) diameter are to be filled.

Precast Concrete

Precast concrete consists of molding concrete elements face down in a controlled environment prior to incorporating them in a structure. In the case of facing material, the finish quality is improved using this method; gravitational force and the short path length enables

air bubbles to easily rise through the liquid concrete, which together with controlled preparation compaction and curing produces high-quality concrete with crisp edges and a

right and below University Library in Utrecht, 2004. Fabrication of rubber mold for precast concrete panels and façade detail.

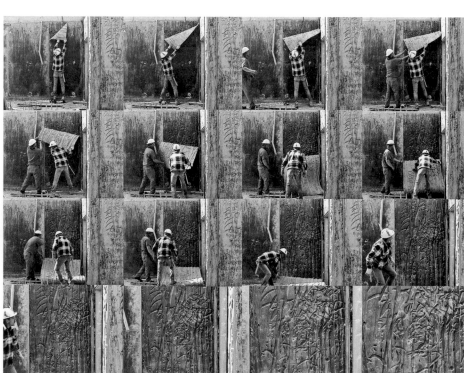

above The Phaeno Science Center, Wolfsburg, Germany, 2005, was constructed with cast-in-place concrete (left side of photo) as well as precast concrete panels. With time the color variation is expected to go away.

smooth surface. Precast concrete fabrication typically occurs in a factory setting followed by shipping completed units to the site via trucks. There are size limitations with this method of construction, based on a truck's ability to transport very large pieces. Larger panels can be cast on site and tilted into position. Although precast concrete fascia panels have been around for many years, they continue to improve the quality of fabrication and design of this architectural element. The University Library in Utrecht, the Netherlands, provides an excellent example of the quality that can be achieved with contemporary precast concrete construction.

The design of the University Library in Utrecht, completed in 2004, has a powerful cubic structure of massive appearance as viewed from the exterior. Dutch architect Wiel Arets' design tried to avoid any impressions of an isolated monolith. The glazing had to be printed with a grid of dots to provide an adequate degree of sunscreening for the interior spaces. A regular grid of dots was not acceptable to the designers, so a screen pattern was

developed by artist Kim Zwarts based upon a photograph of willow branches. The concrete panels achieve the same motif in a relief achieved through the use of rubber molds laid in the concrete forms.

By this method, the concrete panels provide a three-dimensional surface quality. The concrete has a smooth black-painted surface. The panels were stylized using four gray tones. The relief for the form was manually cut to a maximum depth of 25mm (1 inch) in a sheet of polyurethane. Each gray tone was allotted its own separate plane.

The concrete surface was colored. However, colored pigments in the concrete mix were not used because of cost and potential variations in surface tone. The concrete surface was painted after it had set. Two coats of paint were applied to the interior panels and three coats to the exposed panels of the building.

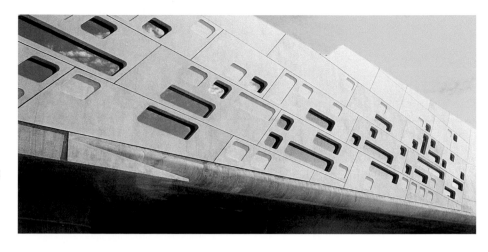

page 60 The self-compacting concrete elements at the Phaeno Science Center, Wolfsburg, which were constructed on site have a fair amount of surface defects at some difficult transitions.

right and below The factory constructed precast concrete panels at the Phaeno Science Center are close to perfect.

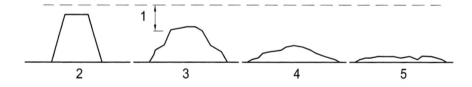

Strength and Workability.
1 In concrete the slump is measured as the distance the concrete settles.
2 Too much sand makes the mix unworkable and sets up too quickly.
3 The ideal slump for traditional concrete is 100 to 150mm (4 to 6 inches)
4 In traditional concrete too much slump will produce weak concrete.
5 SCC produces maximum slope without compromising strength.

Self-compacting Concrete

Self-compacting concrete (SCC) was first developed in Japan in 1988 to reduce labor costs in the placement of concrete. As the name suggests, self-compacting concrete achieves full compaction due to its self-weight. Consolidation is an inherent property of the mix and hence no vibration is required during concrete pouring. Combining high strength with an extremely fluid mix, self-compacting concrete provides a method of producing concrete shapes that would otherwise be impossible to achieve. Like honey on toast, the new material in its liquid stage can fill complex geometric molds, even with dense steel reinforcement. The polycarboxylate ether superplasticizer provides the required flow characteristics. Once the material has hardened it attains high strengths, in the range of 60–100 MPa (8.7–14.5 ksi). Ultra-high performance self-compacting concrete (UHPSCC) has strength characteristics in excess of 150 MPa (21.8 ksi).

The Phaeno Science Center in Wolfsburg, Germany, completed in 2005, used this material to achieve amorphic forms cast in the field with self-compacting concrete. The asymmetric voided slab ceiling was intended to merge into the cones without any transition zones or color differences. The surfaces of the cones reveal the wood grain from the formwork and the formwork connections. Practice for the aboveground cones was possible through trial pores in the underground car park, using cones that are not highly visible to the public. Attention to detail by the design team required that the boards be tapered to reinforce the cone shape of the form. Although not obvious to the eye, the boards were trapezoidal in shape, not rectangular, and the nail positions on the boards were arranged in a regular pattern. The prefabricated formwork elements were artificially aged on-site with a cement wash, in order to provide a consistent appearance to the concrete after the forms were removed. The wax-based formwork release agent was spray-applied prior to pouring.

Curing is particularly important to the finish of self-compacting concrete. The Phaeno Science Center battled with trying to provide uniform color and texture for an incredibly complicated building form. The goal was to have everything in the same high-quality surface finish. The cement mix was closely monitored to obtain consistency in color and texture. The surface finish can resemble an elephant skin if the concrete mixture is not kept in constant motion during pouring. For this reason, the mix was pumped into the forms.

above and below Mexican Embassy, Berlin, 2001. Like a curtain billowing through an open window, the warped plane implied by the pillars directs pedestrians toward the entrance.

page 63 Existing concrete columns match finish of new concrete columns by sand-blasting all columns. Dulles International Airport Expansion, Washington, D.C., 1999.

Fiber-reinforced Concrete

Concrete is a relatively brittle material and will crack if exposed to tensile forces. Since the mid-1800s, steel reinforcing has been used to overcome this problem. Acting as a composite system, the properly located reinforcing steel provides the tensile strength necessary for structural stability. It was discovered that by adding fibers to the concrete mix its inherent tensile strength can be increased by as much as five times. A variety of different fibers can be used according to the material properties required. As a result, tensile forces due to shrinkage or thermal movement can be resisted by the fiber-reinforced concrete.

Finishing Treatments in Concrete

Many surface defects in concrete can be hidden by finishing treatments. Each finishing treatment provides a different effect, but with certain limitations. Finishing of concrete surfaces can take place during the curing process or after the concrete has fully cured. It is important to consider the impact that the choice of finishing treatment has on the integrity of the concrete cover. This relatively thin layer provides the required surface durability, and the designer must select any finishing technique with this in mind. The following is a list of selected surface finishes that can be used to minimize the effects of surface defects.

Sandblast Finish

Sandblasting today is generally carried out using abrasive materials other than sand, its silica dust being dangerous to health. By using an abrasive, fired at the surface by a compressed air jet, concrete can be cleared of dirt, rust, and small surface defects. A sandblast finish is often used to provide a uniform appearance on a surface marked with defects. A classic example of this method of finishing is the expansion of the Dulles International Airport in Washington, D.C, undertaken in 1999. The terminal expansion consisted of extending the 1962 structure at both ends, essentially doubling the size of the building. The original innovative structural form was reused for the expansion. Although unchanged

from the initial design, stricter building codes mandated a stronger concrete mix and safety glazing. At the end of construction, it was desirable to have the same finish on both the new and the old concrete piers (constructed over 30 years previously). The solution was to sandblast the concrete surfaces of all the piers, thus providing a uniform appearance to all elements.

Bush Hammering

A bush hammer is a traditional hand tool that looks like a hammer with a serrated face containing many pyramid-shaped points. The tool was used to dress concrete or stone surfaces. Today, bush hammer surfaces are created with power-driven equipment. The Mexican Embassy in Berlin, Germany, constructed in 2001, used bush hammering of the concrete surfaces at the main building entrance to emulate this traditional Mexican technique for finishing concrete. 18m (60 foot) tall columns tilted to varying degrees provide a curtain of white concrete leading visitors into the building. The white concrete uses a formula of white cement, marble chips and pulverized marble. By exposing the marble aggregate through bush hammering, the light-reflecting capacity of the concrete is improved and a uniform texture achieved. The thin concrete blades are actually precast concrete, whereas the portal frame was cast in place. The bush hammer finishing technique provided a method of making two different methods of forming concrete look the same.

Exposed Aggregate Concrete

To produce an exposed aggregate (washed out) concrete finish, the aggregates in the mix are exposed by washing out the cement paste at the concrete surface. This is achieved by applying a retarder to the surface of the concrete. The retarder slows hydration of the surface layer of cement, making it less hard than the cement beneath it. The surface layer can then be washed out to reveal the underlying course aggregate particles. A muriatic acid solution may then be applied to further clean and brighten the aggregate particles. The Headquarters of Sozialverband Deutschland in Berlin, completed in 2003, provides a good

example of the uniform appearance of an exposed aggregate concrete finish. The building's colorful shiny windows stand out in a background of textured black concrete. The precast concrete panel finish was achieved by washing out the paste of the precast panels, exposing the crushed fine black basalt aggregate. The design provides precast corner panels that wrap the edges of the building with large thick returns. The corner edge is a sharp crisp line. The edges of the panels were protected during transportation and installation. Because the panels are elevated above the ground floor of the building, they are not vulnerable to chipping.

Polished Concrete

A polished concrete finish is completed after the concrete has cured. Typically, the cement slurry in a concrete mix rises to the surface, covering the aggregate. The polishing process involves removal of the cement slurry that hides the internal composition of the concrete and provides a surface that can resemble a terrazzo floor. Like terrazzo, the polishing process brings out the rich color of the mix components. Polished concrete requires an intense scrutiny of materials and processes. The Kunstmuseum in Vaduz, Liechtenstein, completed in 2000, used polished concrete to make what appears to be a monolithic block at the base of a cliff. The main exhibi-

above and right Exposed aggregate in precast concrete panels, Headquarters of Sozialverband Deutschland, Léon Wohlhage Wernik Architekten, Berlin, 2003.

tion rooms are on the upper floor, covered with skylights, and have no windows to the exterior. The form joints were ground down. Any surface voids along with the wall ties were filled with a matching concrete mix prior to grinding the wall. All details are designed to achieve flush joints over the entire building. In strong contrast to the Salk Institute, this museum design tries to hide any clues as to how the building was formed. The concrete polishing revealed the special stone aggregate, broken black basalt, fine-grained green, red and white Rhine River gravel, against the black pigmented cement. The final effect was a semi-reflective surface that constantly changes with the effects of natural light.

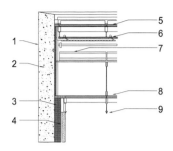

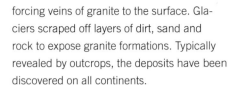

above Section at roof at Kunstmuseum Liechtenstein in Vaduz, 2000.
1 Ground and polished surface
2 Cast-in-place concrete structure, 40cm (15 ³/₄ inches)
3 Foamed glass insulation 14cm (5 ¹/₂ inches)
4 Air space with plaster walls
5 Glass skylight
6 Sunshade lamella
7 Steel support beam
8 Passable glass ceiling
9 Suspended ceiling with perforated plastic sheet

right Kunstmuseum in Vaduz.

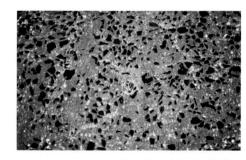

above Kunstmuseum Liechtenstein.

Surface Defects in Stone

Granite is formed from liquid magma, the molten rock found at the core of the earth, cooled slowly to form a substance approaching the hardness and durability of a diamond. Granite is an igneous rock, its chemical compositions similar to lava. However, granite owes its hardness and density to the fact that it has solidified deep within the earth, under extreme pressure. Over the eons, seismic activity has changed the crust of the planet, forcing veins of granite to the surface. Glaciers scraped off layers of dirt, sand and rock to expose granite formations. Typically revealed by outcrops, the deposits have been discovered on all continents.

The rocks that form the earth's crust fall into three generic groups: igneous, sedimentary, and metamorphic. The beauty and durability of these naturally formed rocks bring variation to the architectural form. With these variations come characteristics that can be seen as defects.

Inclusions

An inclusion is the term given to foreign matter in natural stone. Because stone is quarried from the earth, it can have inclusions including metal, carbon, or even shells. Building stone is not typically required to have no inclusions; however, an excess amount can detract from its appearance. The percentage and size of acceptable inclusions should be compared against an established standard so that stone pieces can be accepted or rejected.

above The Walt Disney Concert Hall in Los Angeles, completed in 2003, illustrates the natural color and texture variation natural stone on a wall.

right The Walt Disney Concert Hall, running bond random pattern of stone wall.

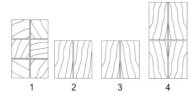

above Traditional veining patterns in stone.
1 Blend pattern
2 Slip pattern
3 Match pattern (also called book-matched)
4 Diamond-matched pattern

below One out-of-place stone can distract from the uniform veining pattern of a stone wall.

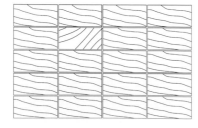

Veining Patterns

The veining in stone is caused by the presence of trace elements at the time of its formation. Iron oxide makes the pinks, yellows, browns and reds. Most gray, blue-gray and black lines are from bituminous substances. These veins are a distinctive part of a stone's appearance and must be considered in the design and installation of the stone. The natural folds and veins found in marble and some granite create distinctive markings throughout the stone. The quarried blocks are cut and finished for particular patterns. Uncontrolled use of natural stone finishes on a building can appear as a visual defect, making it necessary to commit to a pattern when installing the stone. Understanding the veining patterns avoids a break in the overall effect. Traditional veining patterns are: blend, slip, book match, and diamond match.

Fissures and Cracks

Fissures and cracks are natural defects found in some stones. Exotic stones desired for their playful veining and brilliant color are often the materials most affected by these defects. For years, the stone industry has sought to remedy such defects with the use of resins to fill the fissures and cracks; the appearance of a solid piece of stone can then be achieved after surface polishing. Resins are chemical ingredients used to infill surface voids in a stone. Resins give a smooth surface that is difficult to detect in the finished stone; however, they should be used with care.

Resins are not typically stable in an environment exposed to ultraviolet radiation. Fading of resin material can become visible years after an installation has been exposed to direct sunlight. Resin-filled materials can be difficult to refurbish, because the exact material used in the resin can be unknown and therefore difficult to match. Lastly, the chemicals used in resins are not natural and are not always known or tested for surfaces used for the preparation and consumption of food. The use of resin infill for kitchen counter tops is a large controversy in the stone industry.

Surface Defects in Brick and Terracotta

One of the most demanding brick finishes to keep defect-free is sculptured brick. Sculptured brick panels are the most unusual example of customized masonry. The forms are sculptured pieces handcrafted from the green clayware before firing. The unburned units are firm enough to allow the artist to work freely without damage to the brick body, but sufficiently soft for carving, scraping and cutting. After firing, the sculptured surface is permanently set in the brick face. The brick surface can be selected from a variety of textures, including: smooth, wire-cut, stippled, bark and brushed. Defects like chippage, warpage, and cracks in brick are common in

Building Stone Surface Finishes

GEOLOGICAL CATEGORY	COMMON NAME	FINISHES
1. SEDIMENTARY	Sandstone Limestone Dolomite	A) Smooth (machine finished by saw, finder or planner) B) Machine tooled (with uniform grooves) C) Chat sawn (non-uniform) D) Shot sawn (irregular and uneven markings) E) Split face (concave-convex) F) Rock face (convex)
2. METAMORPHIC	Marble Serpentine Onyx Slate[1] Quartzite[1] Gneiss[2] Travertine[4]	A) Sanded B) Honed C) Polished D) Wheel abraded E) Bush hammered F) Split face G) Rock face
3. IGNEOUS	Granite Syenite Diorite[3] Gabbro Andesite Basalt	A) Sawn B) Honed C) Polished D) Machine tooled (four-cut, six-cut, chiseled, axed, ponted, etc.) E) Flammed (also called thermal) F) Sand finished G) Split face H) Rock face

1 Slate and quartzite cannot be polished.
2 Gneiss will take all of the finishes of marble and may also be flame finished.
3 Diorite will not take flame finish.
4 Travertine is actually a limestone but is classified with marbles for surface finishes. Travertine finishes include filled, partially filled, and unfilled.

Sculptured brick free of defects, exterior wall of Zoo Berlin.

the industry, but can be eliminated by visual inspection and testing.

Visual Inspection

After leaving the kiln, bricks and terra-cotta panels are cooled and inspected for chips and color variation. Rejected material is either sold as "seconds" or ground up and mixed with clay to be used in another production run. Some chipping of masonry can go undetected through the fabrication process, or bricks may be damaged by shipping and handling. It is up to the mason to make the final review of bricks prior to building them into the wall. The International Masonry Institute allows no chips or cracks that are visible when viewed from a distance of not less than 6m (20 feet) under diffused lighting.

Brick Testing

Ancient brickmakers took clay from the ground, mixed it with water, shaped it like bread dough into oblong units, and let it air-dry in the sun. Today, brick construction is far more sophisticated and the performance requirements for the bricks are much more stringent. Compression strength and absorption are directly related to the durability of masonry. In addition to inspection of the surface appearance of the bricks, quality testing is essential for ensuring material durability and avoiding future surface defects. Bricks are made with raw materials that possess a natural level of variation. Typically, the desired higher compression strengths and lower absorption rates of brick are linked not only to the raw materials used, but also to higher kiln firing temperatures. For this reason, bricks are laboratory-tested to verify water absorption, compression strength, and efflorescence. Freeze-thaw testing is required for bricks to be used in severe weathering regions. Tests are conducted on a yearly basis for each type of brick and a certificate of test and authenticity is then issued. Architects can require that testing be completed for the run of brick to be used for a specific project; however, this is not typical.

Ando Concrete, Pulitzer Foundation, St. Louis, 2003.

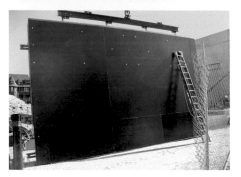

Fabrication of wood forms at Pulitzer Foundation, St. Louis.

How Can Surface Defects Be Avoided and Repaired?

In the architectural community, a concrete material of the highest quality is typically referred to as "Ando Concrete." Tadao Ando, the world-renowned Japanese architect, has been a catalyst for perfecting the art of cast-in-place concrete in projects around the world. Famous for the finished quality of his walls, visitors have to use restraint not to stroke the surface of the silky smooth walls. The Pulitzer Foundation of the Arts in St. Louis, Missouri, completed in 2003, is a good example of how Ando has been able to maintain very high standards outside of his home country. Built as a museum to house the Pulitzer family's art collection, the building also acts as a headquarters for the charitable foundation. A goal of the foundation is to foster an understanding between modern art and architecture. The building has a simple form, two elongated rectangles, each 7.5m (24 feet) wide, are placed parallel to one another, with a rectangular pool of equal width between them. The interplay of levels and plains works well with the monolithic appearance of cast-in-place concrete. The sparseness of detailing allows for greater attention to the finish of the building materials. In order to achieve the high level of finish on the concrete, three aspects of the project had to be mastered: formwork, mix design and pouring procedures.

The concrete's formwork panels were cut and fitted together like bespoke furniture. The forms were made of plastic-coated plywood manufactured in Europe from short grain hardwood material. The panels were butted together tightly. Then the form panels were sealed and polished to a glossy surface. Tie bar cones were custom-made using a hybrid assembled from traditional cones used in the industry. This gave the contractor greater flexibility to uniformly construct a wall of varying thicknesses. The rounding of the tie bar holes is exactly conical. They are precisely sealed with concrete dowels, which are carefully positioned and installed. Nothing is left to chance, from the juxtaposition of board sizes to the arrangement of tie bar holes. The forms were constructed on site in a temporary building and lifted into place by crane. The form release agent was critical to achieving the desired glossy surface finish.

With the architect's desire to create the "perfect concrete," construction crews spent years forming the walls of this single building. The structure had 150 wall pours, which took place over a two-and-a-half-year time period. In order to maintain a uniform appearance the concrete mix was designed with great care. In order to maintain a consistent color on all walls, the raw materials were closely monitored and water levels controlled to obtain a uniform mix for all concrete pours. Higher water levels in concrete can darken the color of the finished material. Merrimac stone was used in the aggregate at the Pulitzer Foundation because it has a very low absorption rate, and is abundant in the region. The mixture went through several trials. The maximum aggregate size was reduced to 19mm ($^3/_4$ inch) in order to improve the strength of the mix at the top of the tall forms.

Timing was critical during concrete placement. The concrete mix used for the project was extremely dense and set quickly, taking approximately two hours to stiffen after being mixed. In order to maintain the quality of color and finish, the time from mixing the material to removing the last vibrator could take no more than two hours. This criterion put enormous pressure on concrete suppliers because the material was mixed off-site at the supplier's plant and delivered by truck. Concrete skips were positioned using cranes and provided just enough material to fill to the top of the formwork. Many men were required to vibrate the concrete in order to ensure compaction. The architect has said that the shine on the surface of the concrete was a reflection of the skill of the people that put it there. Even with the highest quality control during construction, defects occurred. At the Pulitzer Foundation, a total of three walls were replaced after curing because of imperfections. This attention to detail produced finished monolithic planes that deserve the description "Ando concrete."

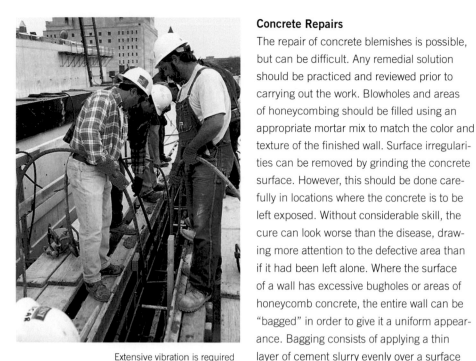

Extensive vibration is required during pours to remove air pockets that can lead to surface defects. Pulitzer Foundation, St. Louis.

Concrete mock-up for Lincoln Park Zoo, Regenstein Center for African Apes, Chicago, 2004.

Concrete Repairs

The repair of concrete blemishes is possible, but can be difficult. Any remedial solution should be practiced and reviewed prior to carrying out the work. Blowholes and areas of honeycombing should be filled using an appropriate mortar mix to match the color and texture of the finished wall. Surface irregularities can be removed by grinding the concrete surface. However, this should be done carefully in locations where the concrete is to be left exposed. Without considerable skill, the cure can look worse than the disease, drawing more attention to the defective area than if it had been left alone. Where the surface of a wall has excessive bugholes or areas of honeycomb concrete, the entire wall can be "bagged" in order to give it a uniform appearance. Bagging consists of applying a thin layer of cement slurry evenly over a surface prior to rubbing it down with a crumpled cement bag. When using this method of covering defects, care should be taken to ensure that the durability of the structure is not affected. Like plaster work, repairs to concrete can be as much an art as a technique and success can vary depending on the experience of the applicator.

Mock-up Samples

Concrete, masonry and stone have surface quality limitations that must be understood by all parties involved in a project. The best way to avoid disappointment with finished components is to specify a representative mock-up for the project. The mock-up should exactly reproduce all details that will be executed on the project, from corner details to wall to ceiling transitions. Stone panels should show all representative veining, color and inclusions that are expected from the selected stone. It is important for designers to specify a repair sample for all finished concrete, together with the repair procedure. Damage is inevitable on a construction site, and repairs will invariably be required. A completed mock-up, accepted by all parties as the representative quality expected on the project, will prevent arguments during construction.

Discoloration

Architects may envisage their buildings as having the coat of a white stallion and be disappointed when finished surfaces take on the motley appearance of a pinto. With exposed construction materials like concrete, maintaining uniformity of color is extremely important. Color differences in concrete have several causes, from variation in mix design to curing methods. Uniformity can be achieved; however, tight quality control of construction materials and methods is required.

Natural stone comes out of the ground with a certain color. That color is typically altered by the finishing applied to the material. For example, a polished finish takes on a different color when compared to a thermal finish. The color can change even more through unwanted staining. Some stains are permanent and can be remedied only by replacing the stone. Natural stone staining can be avoided by protecting it from harmful building products and construction materials. Ironically, one of the most damaging stains comes from water. Designers must carefully consider how water runs off the face of a building. Rainwater can streak buildings with unwanted dirt and chemicals in unexpected locations. Although building maintenance plays its part, good design can make a façade age well.

Color variation can be desirable. Stains and color changes are then planned and welcome. These are projects that challenge the elements with a clear understanding of the limits and attributes of their enclosure. Selecting the correct material and finish for a particular building is critical to preventing disappointment.

The church Dio Padre Misericordioso in Rome, also known as the Jubilee Church, was completed in 2003 to celebrate the third millennium. It is surrounded by 1970s apartment blocks in the suburb of Tor Tre Teste, about 10km (6 miles) east of the center of Rome. The structure houses a main sanctuary, seating approximately 250 people, a chapel and a baptistery. Three self-supporting concrete

shells, symbolizing the Holy Trinity of the Roman Catholic Church, are the focal point of the exterior façade. Soaring from a travertine stone plaza, the concrete walls, formed as segments of a sphere, range in height from 17.4m to 27.4m (57 to 90 feet). The sail-like forms were actually constructed as 10.9 tonne (US short 12 ton) precast concrete elements that were lifted into place. The curved panels provide shelter from direct sun shining into the church. To prevent the panels from discoloring, brilliantly white cement incorporating photocatalytic particles was used in the concrete mix. This special mixture of concrete was intended to neutralize atmospheric pollutants, keeping the panels brilliantly white.

Close inspection of the outside surface of the panels reveals levels of discoloration. Unlike white marble, glass or coated aluminum, the concrete has changed in color just two years after the building was completed. The surfaces that have been exposed to sun, rain, pollutants and temperature swings have become blotchy. What was once an even white concrete shell has turned into a quilt pattern of different shades of white. In strong contrast, the interior side of the shells has

Three self-supporting concrete shells, symbolizing the Holy Trinity of the Roman Catholic Church, are the focal point of the exterior façade. Jubilee Church, Rome, 2003.

above What was once an even white concrete shell has turned into a quilt pattern of different shades of white.

right In strong contrast, the interior side of the shells has maintained its original brilliant white color and finish. Jubilee Church.

ple of curved white aluminum panels that have withstood the test of time and remain brilliantly white on all elevations. The discoloration of the exterior concrete of the Jubilee Church is minor; however, other forms of discoloration can be much more dramatic.

Discoloration of Concrete

When concrete is exposed to view, architects typically desire a uniform color and texture. Many times they are disappointed when an uneven color develops. "Pinto concrete" describes the large, irregularly shaped, dark-colored blotches on the surface of concrete. Typically a problem with flatwork, the Portland Cement Association has documented several common causes of surface discoloration in concrete. Each factor must be considered in order to achieve the required finish.

Water-Cement Ratio
The change to the water-cement ratio of a concrete mix can dramatically affect the color of the concrete. A high water-cement ratio will produce a lighter-colored concrete as compared to a darker color of the same mix with a low water-cement ratio. Although the mix may have the same water-cement ratio in the delivery truck, variations can occur after the concrete is poured. For example, if the grade is not uniformly moistened prior to pouring a concrete slab on grade, localized dry spots can reduce the water-cement ratio in the mix and cause localized discoloration.

The Getty Center in Los Angeles, 1997, provides a good example of curved white aluminum panels that have withstood the test of time and remain brilliantly white on all elevations.

right Raw materials used in concrete can absorb additional water when uncovered in a construction yard. This additional water can slightly affect the color of raw concrete.

maintained its original brilliant white color and finish. Like many contemporary projects, the exposed concrete at Jubilee Church is not painted, but was designed with the expectation that the concrete mix would sustain the desired intense white appearance.

Other buildings have maintained a uniform white appearance by using white aluminum panels with coatings that have been tested and are warranted against fading. The Getty Center in Los Angeles provides a good exam-

The Pinakothek der Moderne, an art museum in Munich, completed in 2002, appears to have discoloration caused by concrete consolidation issues. The underside of the roof slab is exposed to view at the main entrance.

The Pinakothek der Moderne.

right Concrete Discoloration. A change in cement type or the percentage of water in a mix can create a shift in the color.

Cement

Individual brands and types of cement may differ in color depending on the source of the raw material. A change in the type of cement used during a project can cause a noticeable color change in the concrete. If consistent color is desired for a large project, a uniform source of cement should be obtained prior to starting the work.

Calcium Chloride

Calcium chloride is an admixture used to accelerate the curing time of concrete. Great care should be taken with calcium chloride admixtures as relatively little chloride will cause corrosion of embedded steel reinforcement in moist conditions. In addition, calcium chloride or admixtures containing calcium chloride can darken a concrete surface. A mottled appearance of light or dark spots can result, depending on how the concrete is cured and on the alkali content of the cement. Repeated washing or weathering of the concrete can lesson this defect; however, light spots can be particularly difficult to remove and may require a chemical wash to improve uniformity. Light spots on a dark background can be caused by a low alkali to calcium chloride ratio. Dark spots on light background are formed by a high alkali to calcium chloride ratio. Spots can also be caused by coarse aggregate particles located just below the surface of the concrete. This type of discoloration is known as "aggregate transparency." The coarse aggregate can interfere with the surface mortar's chloride content by blocking the normal upward migration of chloride salts to the drying surface. Water ponding of slabs and the use of membrane curing compounds can reduce the amount of discoloration caused by chlorides in a concrete pour.

The East Wing of the National Gallery of Art in Washington, D.C., competed 1978. The architectural concrete is composed of white cement, a coarse pink aggregate, a fine white aggregate and marble dust from the same Tennessee quarries that provided stone for the exterior cladding.

The East Wing of the National Gallery of Art.

Mineral Admixtures

Similar to the effect of mixing paint, colored mineral admixtures will affect the color of the final mix. For example, dark gray fly ash will give concrete a darker color, whereas tan- or beige-colored fly ashes will produce a tan-colored concrete. Silica fume can give concrete a dark gray tint.

Aggregates

The choice of aggregates will affect the color of the finished concrete. For example, white sand can produce uniform white-colored concrete. Dark areas can occur over coarse aggregate particles near the surface. Aggregates containing contaminates such as iron oxides and sulfides can cause unsightly rust stains if they are located near the surface of concrete. The formed concrete ceiling and large concrete lintels of the East Wing of the National Gallery of Art in Washington, D.C., have a similar color to the Tennessee marble used to clad the building.

Trowel burn occurs when hard troweling of a concrete surface is executed after the concrete has become too stiff.

The San Nicola Stadium in Bari in the South of Italy, 1990, shows color differentiation across the concrete surface. Variation in the absorption of forms or inconsistent application of the form release agent can cause this type of discoloration.

Finishing

The finishing of a concrete slab can greatly affect its color. Hard-steel troweling reduces the water-cement ratio of the surface concrete, resulting in a darker color. Trowel burn occurs when hard troweling of a concrete surface is executed after the concrete has become too stiff to be troweled properly. It can cause extreme discoloration by significantly reducing the water-cement ratio at the surface. Metal abrasion on the surface of the concrete can be an indication of the effect. Trowel burns are extremely difficult to remove; therefore, timely finishing of the concrete is critical to maintaining uniform color.

Curing

Proper curing is essential for concrete. Great care should be taken to ensure not only that curing produces the optimum concrete quality from a mix, but also that unwanted discoloration doesn't occur. Discoloration of a concrete surface can be the result of procedures or compounds used in the curing process. Plastic films are often used to maintain moisture levels when curing concrete. The evaporation and condensation of water at different points under a plastic film can cause discoloration in the curing process. Known as the "greenhouse effect," water condenses under folds in the film and runs down to collect in low spots where the plastic film is in contact with the concrete. Because the concrete surface is exposed to varying water contents and thus non-uniform curing, slight to extreme discoloration in the finish of the concrete can occur. This type of discoloration is typically associated with concrete mixtures containing calcium chloride. The "greenhouse effect" can be avoided by uniformly wetting the concrete as it cures. If a plastic film is used during curing, it should be laid as flat as possible over the concrete.

Efflorescence

Efflorescence is a white crystalline deposit that can develop on new concrete. Water in wet hardened concrete contains dissolved salts (usually a carbonate). As the salt-water solution evaporates, salts may be left on the surface. Efflorescence can typically be removed with a dry brushing and will not persist provided the salt-water solution and evaporation are limited.

Forms

In a cast-in-place wall, the forms used to hold the concrete during hardening can greatly influence the color and texture of the concrete. Forms with different rates of absorption produce different shades of color. For example, unsealed wood forms will absorb moisture from the concrete, which causes dark-colored surfaces due to the reduced water-cement ratio. Sealed, non-absorbing forms will lighten surfaces of concrete, as water levels remain high during the curing process. Discoloration caused by varying absorption rates can also be triggered by non-uniform application of release agents to the forms, as can a change in the type or brand of form release agent during a project. Forms that separate or pull away from the concrete surface, allowing air to come in contact with the surface, can cause a drying discoloration of the exposed area.

If formwork panel joints are not tight and sealed, water and cement paste may ooze out of the joints, creating defects in the hardened concrete (see the "Surface Defects" chapter for more details). The loss of water causes a reduction in the water-cement ratio near the leaking joint, resulting in a darker color. When forms are used repeatedly for separate pours, it can be difficult to maintain tight well-sealed joints.

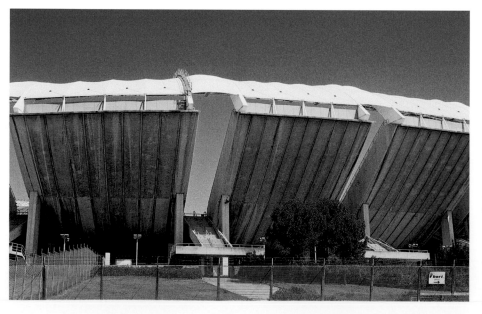

Release agents

A separating film known as a release agent prevents adhesion between formwork and concrete. Release agents ease the tasks of cleanly stripping formwork from the concrete component and of cleaning the formwork surface. A highly effective release agent will produce a better quality surface. It is important to make sure that particles of loose dirt, rust flakes, and construction debris are not deposited onto the film as this can lead to color changes of the finished concrete surface. Release agents can be oils, waxes, paints and emulsions. Pure mineral oil release agents tend to leave residues on the formwork. They are typically used in applications where higher levels of surface finish quality are not required. For the best finish the release agent must not accumulate unevenly on the formwork. It is also important that the products used are waterproof in case bad weather delays concrete pouring during the construction process.

Contemporary Arts Center, Cincinnati, Ohio, 2003. Colored concrete on the building façades differentiates the shifting volumes.

right above Contemporary Arts Center. Unintentionally, the concrete that bears the building's name appears to have been cast with a different method than the other panels adjacent to it.

right Met Lofts, Los Angeles, completed in 2006 by the firm Johnson Fain. Surface discoloration on exterior concrete walls is intentionally left untouched to provide an urban feel to the façade. Stains resulting from the form release agent and efflorescence have not been removed.

A pink color can occur on a formed surface if the forming material or release agent contains phenolics. The phenolics react with the alkali hydroxide solutions in the fresh concrete to cause staining. The best way to prevent this is to use a non-staining release agent on wood forms that have been properly sealed with a non-phenolic sealer. The pink stain generally disappears after a few weeks of air-drying. Coloration of concrete is not always a problem; indeed, in some cases it is the desired effect.

Colored Concrete

In many cases concrete is intentionally colored to provide contrast in a façade. Cincinnati's Contemporary Arts Center, completed in 2003, was designed around the concept of an "urban carpet" to draw in pedestrian traffic

right and below Ruffi Gymnasium, Marseilles, 2001. The patchwork of differently toned concrete panels on the façade provides a deliberately patterned effect. The panel colors were achieved by applying different types of varnish to the concrete surface.

below right Ruffi Gymnasium. The reflection of St. Martin's Church is appropriately visible in the unique window.

from the downtown streets of Cincinnati. Layers of concrete begin outside at the base of the building and unfold through the interior spaces. Colored concrete on the building façades further differentiates the shifting volumes. Coloring is achieved by including a pigment in the mix. Uncolored panels bearing the name of the museum appear to be unintentionally darker in color. The origin of this color shift may be related to this particular panel being constructed at a later date than the rest of the adjacent panels on the façade. In an effort to avoid issues of non-uniformity of concrete, some projects choose to exaggerate discoloration.

The Ruffi Gymnasium, completed in 2001 in Marseilles, by Rémy Marciano, provides an excellent solution to the natural variation that can be experienced between concrete pours. Adjacent to the St. Martin's Church, the semi-industrial nature of the gym design is contextual with the semi-industrial, shed vernacular of the region. The concrete panels on the exterior of the building provide privacy and durability for three interconnecting gyms. Instead of trying for a uniform finish, the concrete is treated to accentuate differences between different pours. The patchwork of dif-

Guggenheim Museum, New York, was completed shortly after Frank Lloyd Wright died, in 1959.

Guggenheim Museum, New York. The façade is frequently in disrepair and needs to be painted every four years.

toric works have often struggled with painted concrete. The Guggenheim Museum, New York, was completed shortly after Frank Lloyd Wright died, in 1959. This building has had a continual problem with the exterior paint. The façade is frequently in disrepair and needs to be painted every four years. These problems could be related to the surface preparation of the concrete or to the coating used to cover it. New painting products have been developed which provide a longer-lasting elastomeric solution for buildings. The painting industry today has a variety of products to provide a uniform appearance to concrete. Some paint products can be classified as stains because they penetrate the surface of the material. A stain is thus integral to the concrete and does not peel off. Light-tinted stains will maintain a certain amount of color variation that may be desired in the finished product.

Chemical Staining

Concrete surfaces can be chemically stained to give variations in color and texture. The Mustakivi School and Community Center in Helsinki uses chemically stained precast concrete panels to break up the uniformity of a complex of buildings clad with precast concrete sandwich panels. The exterior panels of the school block form a load-bearing structure, which supports precast floor planks at the first floor and roof level. The precast sandwich panels consist of two internally connected concrete wythes separated by an insulated core. The colors on the external panel surface represent a canvas of abstract art, of neutral tones and regular shapes arranged in an asymmetric design. Not all of the surface colors are even; some panels are rusty gold in appearance, some look green with wood stain, and some are yellow in color. The basic earth colors of iron oxides and copper sulphides are particularly interesting. This project refutes the notion that concrete sandwich panels have to be boring. The chemical stain is a very thin layer on the surface of the concrete panel. The stain is durable under exposure to rain or snow, but cannot withstand heavy abrasion. A surface treatment of commercial sealant was used to avoid dirt and unwanted graffiti penetrating the concrete micro-pores of the panel surface. The appearance of chemical staining

ferently toned concrete panels on the façade provides a deliberately patterned effect. The panel colors were achieved by applying different types of varnish to the concrete surface.

Painting Concrete

Painting can provide a uniform appearance to concrete. It can also be useful for covering defects due to construction or vandalism. Furthermore, a painted surface will provide protection for reinforced concrete, depending on the paint formulation. The concrete works of Santiago Calatrava are many times painted to give the structure a uniform appearance. Coatings have varied in performance through the years and have not always been effective in adhering to a concrete substrate. Great his-

The Mustakivi School and Community Center in Helsinki, 1998, designed by ArkHouse, uses chemically stained precast concrete panels for non-uniform earthy tones.

below Precast concrete sandwich panels, Mustakivi School and Community Center.
1 Exterior wythe panel is chemically stained
2 Interior wythe provides for building structure

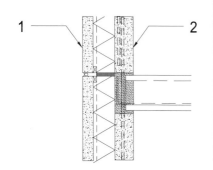

is largely dependent on the absorbency of the concrete surface and its pore structure. Installation requires a certain amount of artistry and can be much more labor-intensive than standard pigmented concrete.

The apparition of the Virgin Mary was caused by a water stain on a concrete wall. Chicago, 2005.

The staining of concrete can be seen by some groups as not only beautiful, but divine. In April 2005, the water stains on a concrete wall under a Chicago highway became a small pilgrimage location for hundreds of kneeling visitors. Many believe that the stain was not just water mixed with salts leaking through the underpass wall from the highway above, but the apparition of the Virgin Mary created to console the world for the loss of Pope John Paul II. The stained concrete became a place of worship for many Christians in Chicago. Although this image was only visible for a few months, the coloration of concrete through a chemical process can create permanent images that will remain on the surface of a structure for many years.

Eberswalde Technical School, built in Eberswalde near Berlin, in 1999.

Concrete can be photo-engraved through a process similar to silk-screening. Eberswalde Technical School.

Photoengraved Concrete

Concrete can be photoengraved through a process similar to silk-screening. A photo is screen-printed as a layer of tiny dots onto a polystyrene sheet, but instead of using paint or ink, the image is printed with a cure retarder liquid. A cure retarder is a chemical that slows the cure rate of concrete. The prepared sheet is then placed into the concrete mold and the concrete poured on top of it. When the concrete has set, it is removed from the mold and pressure-washed, revealing a half-tone image on the finished concrete surface. Eberswalde Technical School, designed by Herzog and de Meuron, used photoengraved concrete to provide detail to what would otherwise be a flat concrete box. The photoengraved pattern was also applied to the glass using a silkscreen coating technique. The concrete impression process has proven to be very successful, retaining its color and detail many years after completion. Like many finished surfaces, a regular pattern of color variation can hide any slight discoloration of the surface. The discoloration of materials is not limited to concrete. Natural stone can also have shifts in color that are not anticipated.

The concrete impression process has proven to be very successful, retaining its color and detail many years after completion.

The East Wing of the National Gallery of Art, in Washington, D.C., has the most famous example of stained stone in the history of modern architecture.

below The Washington Monument in Washington, D.C., shows a clear demarcation in the sculpture from when the work stopped and started again.

Woman touching the National Gallery of Art sharp corner.

Discoloration of Natural Stone

Many natural stones exhibit variations in color and texture. Stone is after all a natural material quarried from the ground. The Washington Monument in Washington, D.C., serves as a reminder of how the color of stone can vary. Construction of the monument started in 1836 but was halted during the American Civil War. After the war, work continued on the monument. There is a clear demarcation in the sculpture from when the work stopped and started again. The color shift could be attributed to a change in the location of the quarry supplying the stone, or to discoloration that occurred between halting the project and the completion time. This element of discoloration tells an important story about the history of the monument and of the United States. Other interesting forms of stone discoloration can be seen in the city of Washington, D.C.

Staining of Stone

The East Wing of the National Gallery of Art, in Washington, D.C., designed by architect I. M. Pei, has the most famous example of stained stone in the history of modern architecture. The sleek, angular modernism of the museum, completed in 1978, is in strong contrast to the neoclassical design of the 1941 Natural Gallery of Art just to the west. Both designs use the same Tennessee pink marble to enclose their walls; both, however, take on completely different forms. In 1986, The American Institute of Architects, College of Fellows, designated the East Wing for the National Gallery of Art as one of the ten most successful examples of architectural design in the United States. The famous solid corner pieces have provided the architectural community with an icon. Visitors touch the corner both in tradition and genuine curiosity leaving one famous stain. A similar stain occurs inside the building on a sign carved in stone that bears the building architect's name. The East Wing walls consist of exterior blocks of stone supported by stainless steel connections from concrete and brick core walls averaging 30cm (12 inches) in thickness. Neoprene strips between blocks allow for expansion and contraction while eliminating the

need for sealant or mortar joints. This design detail reduces the need for maintenance through failed sealant joints or tuckpointing. The typical stone joints for this project are not in contact with any sealant.

Contact with certain sealants can often cause discoloration of stone. The silicone oil or plasticizers used to improve the elastic modulus

above The finish of the stone changed between completion of the original building and the time it was expanded. The difference comes partly from the algae growth. Eiteljorg Museum of American Indians and Western Art, Indianapolis.

page 82 above Neoprene strips between stone blocks open up at locations where the stone blocks have shifted. The East Wing of the National Gallery of Art.

page 82 below Similar to the exterior corner, a stain occurs inside the building on a sign carved in stone that bears the building architect's name. The East Wing of the National Gallery of Art.

(ability to expand and contract) of certain sealants and primers can lead to staining of the stone. Porous materials exposed to sealants with a high plasticizer content will be stained. Oil-based caulks are not recommended for use with limestone. Many butyl sealants can stain stone, and the most common occurrence of this problem is contact with high-modulus silicone. Uncured silicone oil can leach into the stone, permanently discoloring the material. The collection of dirt on silicone sealant and horizontal projections can also lead to staining of stone. As rainwater washes over these features, it can deposit excessive amounts of dirt on isolated areas of the wall. This concentrated streaking can lead to unwanted staining. Water runoff can be a major source of staining on concrete, stone and masonry buildings.

Natural Discoloration

Indiana and Indianapolis were named after their first human inhabitants. Completed in 1989, the Eiteljorg Museum of American Indians and Western Art, pays tribute to this group. The 10,960m² (118,000 square feet) honey-colored museum is composed of nearly 12,000 pieces of hand-cut Minnesota dolomite, a stone creating the feel of the Southwestern Pueblo. Plum-colored German sandstone serves as the building's base. It was decided to allow algae to decorate the museum walls. In 2005, construction of the Mel and Joan Perelman Wing doubled the size of the institution. The new north end of the museum faces the Indianapolis Center Canal. The finish of the stone changed between completion of the original building and the time it was expanded. The difference comes partly from the algae growth. If algae discoloration is not wanted in heavily planted wetted areas, application of a water repellent coating should be considered. These coatings form a hydrophobic layer that requires renewal every two to three years as its effect reduces with time. If an alga is to be allowed to build up on concrete surfaces, the cover to steel reinforcement must be thicker. Other forms of natural discoloration are less desirable than growth of algae on the Eiteljorg Museum of American Indians and Western Art.

Completed in 1989, the Eiteljorg Museum of American Indians and Western Art pays tribute to this group.

Hall Auditorium at Oberlin College, Ohio, 1953.

The top portion of the undulating stone façade has marks from a soffit that does not drip water away from the façade. Hall Auditorium at Oberlin College.

Water Runoff

Uncontrolled water runoff on a building can leave hideous stains on a façade. Examples of water-runoff stains can be found in every major city in the world. Completed in 1953, Hall Auditorium, at Oberlin College, Ohio, provides a good example of how white marble can be permanently stained from run-off water. The top portion of the undulating stone façade has marks from a soffit that does not drip water away from the façade. Water runoff can be attributed to poor design or poor building maintenance.

Properly detailed drip edges can direct water away from wall surfaces, protecting them from discoloration. If no drips are provided, water marks will be present on dark surfaces as well as light ones. The headquarters of the Berlin Water Works, House III was constructed in 2000, in strong contrast to the neighboring Baroque buildings of Berlin. The five-story façade is composed of broken, prism-like forms the color of granite and is based on the styles of Cubism. Water stains can be seen at the changes of the planes of the façade.

Water stains can be seen at the changes of the planes of the façade. The headquarters of the Berlin Water Works, House III Close up.

The headquarters of the Berlin Water Works, House III, 2003.

Light-colored concrete shows the worst stains. Water runoff from large horizontal surfaces can carry extensive amounts of dirt down the face of a building. The Federal Chancellery building, completed in Berlin in 2001, was part of a "ribbon" of government buildings running along the River Spree, uniting East and West Berlin. This series of buildings is architecturally linked by formal blocks with large circular cut-outs. One façade that faces the River Spree is badly stained from rainwater. The circular cut-out in the façade has a large projecting ledge that collects dirt and other air-borne debris. After rainfall, the water runs off the sill, takes the dirt with it and streaks down the face of the building, discoloring the façade. The forces of nature can permanently stain our buildings; however, the most troublesome marks on a building façade in an urban environment come from human intervention.

right After rainfall, the water runs off the sill, takes the dirt with it and streaks down the face of the building, discoloring the façade. The Federal Chancellery building, Berlin, 2001.

The new Innsbruck Ski Jump, designed by Zaha Hadid and completed in 2002, provides an excellent drip edge at the window sill.

Innsbruck Ski Jump.

Vandalism

In an urban environment, graffiti and other acts of vandalism can discolor exterior walls wherever they are accessible; however, there are ways of protecting the appearance of façades. One method is to make the surface impervious to the markings of vandals. The four exterior walls of the Bregenz Art Museum by Peter Zumthor are composed of shingled, frameless translucent glass covering the entire concrete structure. These details make it difficult to permanently paint or mark the exterior walls of the museum. Paint markings can be scraped off the glass easily. Concrete, stone and masonry surfaces are more porous than glass and require a different strategy.

Anti-graffiti protection can be provided through coatings specially made for concrete, stone, and terra-cotta panels. These coatings often take the form of a very thick paint that prevents the graffiti spray from bonding to the surface. The graffiti is then easy to remove.

above Bregenz Art Museum, Bregenz, Austria, 1997. All-glass walls are less susceptible to graffiti than a porous stone or concrete wall.

page 87 These glass details make it difficult to permanently paint or mark the exterior walls of the museum. Bregenz Art Museum, Bregenz, Austria, 1997.

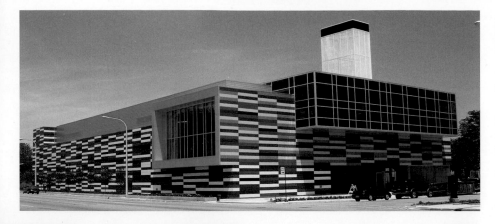

A second strategy to combat vandalism is to make the enclosure panels easily replaceable. The Gary Comer Youth Center was designed by John Ronan Architects to provide practice and performance space for the South Shore Drill Team and Performing Arts Ensemble in Chicago. Completed in 2006, the building is clad with a colorful array of architectural fiber cement façade panels. The panels are approximately 6.25mm (¼ inch) thick and riveted to a metal framing with stainless steel fasteners. Because the building is located in an active urban environment, the design for the building envelope at the street level had to consider the possibility of graffiti on the walls. If panels are discolored beyond repair, they can easily be replaced with panels from stock.

The Gary Comer Youth Center,
Chicago, 2006.

The building is clad with a
colorful array of architectural
fiber cement façade panels.
The Gary Comer Youth Center.

The fiber cement façade
panels can easily be replaced
if damaged from vandalism.
The Gary Comer Youth Center.

The Pulitzer Foundation building in St. Louis provides a
coating of the anti-graffiti project every three years. The
coating is only applied at the
lower level of the building and
is not visible after it has dried.

below IRCAM Music Extension, Paris, 1990. The office
building has been marked
with graffiti. Removal of the
marks has discolored the
terra-cotta panel system.

If left unsealed, some stones can stain due to standing water.

below Staining of stone from contact with sealants can only be avoided by using materials that have been successfully tested for staining with the stone in question.

right Stone replacement is the only method for removing the picture-frame effect of sealant joint stains.

How Can Surface Discoloration Be Avoided and Repaired?

Uniform color in raw cast-in-place concrete can be achieved. The key is to provide consistent ingredients for each pour. A concrete mix typically consists of four major ingredients: cement, course aggregate, sand and water. Because Portland cement is a natural material that can come from a variety of quarries, color consistency can be achieved only by purchasing material that originates from the same source. Maintaining consistent water in the mix can be difficult because the raw materials in concrete are often absorbent and left uncovered in construction yards. A concrete mix containing highly absorbent limestone aggregate can have inconsistent water content in the mix, depending on whether or not the limestone is wet or dry prior to mixing. In addition to maintaining a consistent source of Portland cement for its mix, the Pulitzer Foundation for the Arts in St. Louis, Missouri, provided uniformity in color for the exposed concrete walls by selecting Merrimac stone in lieu of limestone for aggregate. Merrimac is an abundant local stone in the St. Louis area, which could easily be obtained from the same quarry for the entire project. Using 19mm (³/₄ inch) rock, 6.25mm (¹/₄ inch) river gravel, and sand, Merrimac provided a non-absorbent course and fine aggregate for the concrete mix that aided in maintaining a consistent water-cement ratio and thus a more uniform color for the exposed walls.

Remedies for Concrete Discoloration

The Portland Cement Association offers several remedies for improving discolored concrete. These solutions are not necessarily designed for stains caused by spillage or application of foreign substances. The first and typically effective remedy for concrete discoloration is an immediate, thorough flushing of the concrete surface with water. By alternately flushing and drying the concrete surfaces overnight, discoloration can be reduced. Hot water is typically more effective and scrub brushing helps to remove any unsightly surface deposits. A power wash can be a useful alternative to brush scrubbing;

however, this must be done with care so as not to damage the surface of the concrete. If water scrubbing is not effective, acids and other chemicals can be used with care to remove discoloration. A dilute solution of one to two percent to 2% hydrochloric or muriatic acid can be used to remove persistent carbonate efflorescence. Harsh acids can expose the aggregate and should not be used unless this is the desired effect. Acid washing using weaker acids such as three percent acetic acid or three percent phosphoric acid will also remove efflorescence and lessen mottled discoloration caused by uneven curing. Before acid is applied, the surface must be thoroughly dampened with water to prevent the acid from being absorbed deep into the concrete. Treating a dry slab with ten percent solution of caustic soda (sodium hydroxide) gives some success in blending light spots with a dark background. The sodium hydroxide solution should be left on the surface of the concrete for one to two days, followed by a thorough rinsing with water.

The best method for removing most forms of discoloration from concrete is to treat the dry surface with a 20 to 30 percent water solution of diammonium citrate. Treatment consists of applying the solution to the dry surface for about 15 minutes. The white gel formed by the solution should be diluted with water and continuously agitated by brushing. The gel should be scrubbed off with water after the

treatment. Water curing between or after treatments increases the treatment's effectiveness. Typically, two or three treatments will do the job. Acid and other chemical washes should be tested on a small, inconspicuous portion of the discolored concrete to insure the remedy is effective. The cure can, in some cases, be worse than the disease, and care should be taken when experimenting with different techniques and materials. As a general rule, the sooner the remedial methods are applied to discolored concrete, the more effective they will be.

Localized stains on concrete can be treated with muriatic acid; however, it may be necessary to clean all areas of the concrete with the solution in order to provide a uniform appearance. An acid wash, in addition to removing troubling stains, may also remove the calcium carbonate deposits that are normally left on the surface of concrete flatwork. Removing the calcium carbonate along with the stains will reveal the darker underlying concrete. Uniform treatment of all areas will minimize the risk of an uneven finish.

Stone Discoloration

Sealers are used to prevent discoloration of natural stone. Sealers are particularly necessary for stones with high absorptions rates, such as marble. Granite has lower absorption rates; however, for counter tops with a polished finish, sealers need to be periodically reapplied in order to prevent staining of the stone. Staining of stone from contact with sealants can only be avoided by using materials that have been successfully tested for staining with the stone in question. Stone replacement is the only method for removing the picture-frame effect of sealant joint stains. As with concrete, discoloration of stone due to dirty water runoff can be remedied with effective details that drain water away from vertical surfaces of the building. This is particularly important when vertical surfaces are adjacent to large horizontal projections like window sills. Stone that is dirty from water runoff can be cleaned; however, without removing the cause, discoloration is sure to come back.

1

In order to minimize discoloration of concrete, do not use calcium chloride admixtures, but use consistent/uniformly proportioned concrete ingredients. Also use proper, consistent, timely finishing and curing practices. Any disruption or change in the concrete mix, formwork, finishing or curing can result in surface discoloration of the concrete.

2

Some level of variation is to be expected with concrete. Uniformity of concrete color and texture requires consistency of mix and placement. Slight variations can cause dramatic discoloration. Discoloration is typically the result of changes in either the concrete's mix composition or in the method by which the concrete was produced.

3

In order to obtain color uniformity in a concrete mix, quality-control methods must ensure that equivalent materials are used in all pours along with equal water content. Water can be present in absorbent materials used in a mix, or in the surfaces onto which the concrete is poured. Variation in water contact can change the color of the finished product.

4

Paint can be applied to correct discoloration of concrete; however, this type of surface coating will not be as durable as finishes that are integral to the mix.

5

Concrete designs must consider the limitations of all materials used on a project. Exposure to ultraviolet radiation can fade materials with organic pigments. Inorganic materials typically have a better resistance to fading.

6

The staining of concrete can be used as a design feature. Controlled discoloration can provide elegant detail to what would otherwise be a bland, flat façade.

7

Designers must consider how water runs off a building. Uncontrolled water runoff can leave a building streaked with dirt and unsightly stains.

8

Vandalism of building façades in an urban environment must be anticipated. A variety of non-visible solutions exist to protect building elements from graffiti.

Silicone sealant can stain white marble.

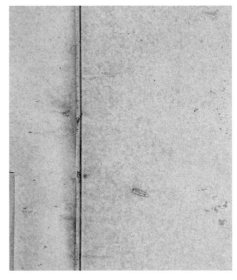

Stone replacement is the only method for removing the picture-frame effect of sealant joint stains.

Corrosion

terra cotta were developed with the birth of skeleton construction methods for high-rise buildings in the late 1800s. Steel-frame construction quickly replaced load-bearing masonry walls at the turn of the century as a means of forming taller buildings. With time these innovative enclosures are showing their age. The symptoms of deterioration include cracked, delaminated, spalled, and displaced sections of masonry. The most common mechanism of failure for these large masonry buildings is the corrosion of the metal fasteners that support the façades.

Contemporary designers are aware of the limited durability of these old walls and have developed new methods of attaching stone cladding that greatly improve corrosion resistance. Today, galvanized steel or stainless steel fasteners are used to secure stone cladding. The aim of these new materials is to improve the life of our building cladding systems by limiting corrosion.

Concrete buildings are not exempt from corrosion problems. The success of contemporary reinforced concrete rests on the tensile force of embedded steel reinforcement. However, without adequate concrete cover, steel reinforcement will corrode with resulting rust stains and concrete spalls, leading ultimately to structural damage. New developments in concrete construction have moved toward

In the summer of 2000, Chicago experienced a series of stone-cladding failures that heightened people's awareness of its deteriorating high-rise masonry buildings. In one incident, large chunks of masonry from Chicago's La Salle Street Building fell to the street, damaging cars. New York City is faced with a similar risk. The root of the problem is found not in the stone, but in the metal connections that tie the stone cladding to the building. This mode of failure may be traced back to the history of construction for these great cities. Masonry cladding systems providing façades in materials such as brick, limestone and

above Removal of the stone cladding reveals the corroded steel structure.

right Corrosion of carbon steel can lead to terrible rust stains.

page 93 Corner conditions experience higher wind loads and thermal expansion, thus requiring the most significant repair work.

greater corrosion resistance. Epoxy-coated steel and stainless steel reinforcement have added additional protection against corrosion, as have improved concrete mixes. New products like fiber-reinforced concrete and fiber-reinforced polymer (FRP) reinforcing bars are aimed at the total elimination of steel reinforcement from concrete. Modern construction methods are tackling corrosion of structures; however, with the introduction of any new product, care must be taken to avoid the possibility of catastrophic failure in years to come.

The masonry industry experienced a corrosion catastrophe in the mid 1970s. A high-tensile-strength mortar additive was developed and marketed under the name Sarabond. Many thought it was a breakthrough in mortar technology. Sarabond was first introduced to the construction market in 1965 as a mortar additive that increased masonry's flexural strength fourfold and its tensile strength threefold over conventional mortar. It was intended to revolutionize the use of brick in high-rise construction. A laboratory cousin of Saran Wrap, Sarabond was intended to make mortar as strong as the bricks it joined. Made of saran latex, it was intended to render mortar less permeable to air and water infiltration, thus protecting any embedded steel from corrosion. The hope was that this new technology would expand the creative possibilities of masonry for architects and engineers. The product was used throughout North America, from the Giraffe House at the Denver Zoo to a United Auto Workers building in Detroit. Sarabond had become a commonplace additive in masonry construction. In 1977, disaster struck as many of the projects that used Sarabond began to have problems. In one case, bricks from the 23-story façade of the Central National Bank in Cleveland, Ohio, came crashing to the street just a few years after the building had been completed. The bank façade was completed in 1970, using over 1.8 million bricks, bonded together with a mortar mix that contained Sarabond. Investigation of the façade and others like it uncovered a problem with Sarabond, and the issue related to corrosion.

In traditional masonry walls, when steel reinforcement is embedded in conventional cementitious mortar, a stable oxide coating is formed over the steel surface, thereby protecting the steel from damaging corrosion. Investigation revealed that the Sarabond additive creates a corrosive environment for embedded steel. Sarabond was a latex modifier containing polyvinyl chloride (PVC). When Sarabond was added to fresh cement, it released chloride into the cement pores. In sufficient concentration, chloride ions destroy the normally protective steel oxide coating that develops naturally over the surface reinforcement in contact with cementitious mortars and concretes; the oxide coating becomes unstable, giving rise to damaging corrosion at the steel surface. As steel corrodes, it gains in volume. In a cementitious mortar, the expansion due to uncontrolled corrosion at the metal surface generates tension forces. Cement mortars have little capacity to resist these tension forces, even with the increased strength characteristics of Sarabond, and cracks develop in the mortar. The combination

right and below Central National Bank, Cleveland, Ohio, 1970. Corrosion of wall reinforcement caused brick walls to fall to the street just seven years after the project was completed.

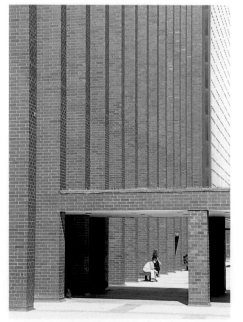

above Giraffe House, Denver Zoo, detail.

right Corrosion of masonry joint. Giraffe House, Denver Zoo.

Open concrete balconies are susceptible to reinforcement corrosion caused by weather and de-icing salts. Marina Towers, Chicago.

of uncontrolled steel corrosion and cracking of the supporting mortar leads eventually to failure of the steel. Where steel fasteners or ties are used, this type of failure can result in buckling of an entire wall of bricks. Sarabond was blamed for weakening the reinforcement system and for causing façades to peel away from the building and bricks to plunge to the street below. In the case of the Central National Bank in Cleveland, the solution was replacement of the brick façade.

The Sarabond problem was not limited to the project in Cleveland. In fact, the effects of Sarabond were felt throughout North America, including Canada. 3080 Yonge Street is a medium-size office building in Toronto, Ontario, which used Sarabond as an admixture for its masonry façade. Similar to the Central National Bank, façade replacement was required. The building owners decided to replace the brick façade with a curtainwall composed of glass and granite. The existing brick walls were removed during the night and the new curtainwall was installed during the day without tenants vacating the space. Test studies revealed that mortar mixtures with Sarabond additive produced considerably more chloride than other mixes, thereby stripping away the protective oxide coating on steel and allowing the corrosion to proceed. The problems related to Sarabond were similar in nature to the problems related to calcium chloride used in the concrete industry.

Calcium Chloride

The addition of small amounts of specific materials to concrete in order to improve the mix property is as old as the use of cement itself. The Romans used blood, pig's fat and milk as additives to pozzolanic cements to improve their workability and durability. In contemporary concrete, many admixtures are used; for example, water reducers, retarders, accelerators, and waterproofers improve different characteristics of the mix. An accelerator increases the rate of set of the concrete mix. Calcium chloride was found to significantly reduce the setting time of concrete when added to concrete mixes as pellets or flakes or solution form. This was particularly useful for projects requiring concrete work in cold temperatures. Because low temperatures increase the setting time, it allowed for faster construction. Regardless of the temperature or cement type, concrete mixes containing calcium chloride will have a faster cure rate than plain concrete. The practice was also adopted by the precast concrete industry as the reduced concrete setting time allowed an increase in output from the available molds. After years of use through the 1960s, calcium chloride had become a common admixture to concrete mixes. It was later determined that chlorides in concrete increased the risk of corrosion of embedded metal. After the completion of many projects, strong recommendations from the industry advised against the use of calcium chloride and chloride-based admixtures in reinforced concrete design. The Brick Institute advised against chlorides as early as 1968, indicating that their use could lead to corrosion of metals.

Although the use of calcium chloride in concrete was halted in the 1970s and the production of Sarabond was stopped in 1982, there is still merit in sharing the story. Architects and engineers must learn from construction history and cautiously subscribe to innovative new products that offer superior performance. Innovation can come at a cost. In the case of Sarabond and calcium chloride, the cost was metal corrosion.

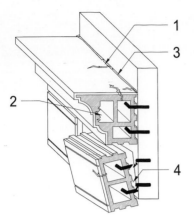

above Failure of terra-cotta panels.

1 Crazing – Fine cracking of the glaze finish due to thermal expansion and contraction of terra cotta. Moisture can enter through the cracks.

2 Spalling – The partial loss of masonry caused by water trapped within the terra-cotta unit.

3 Mortar deterioration – Deteriorated mortar joints are a source of water infiltration.

4 Deterioration of metal anchoring – Deteriorated anchoring system due to water infiltration and rusting of carbon steel anchor can be severe before it is noticed. As a result, terra-cotta blocks can fall from the building with little warning.

above right Terra-cotta panels are susceptible to corrosion failures.

right Close-up inspection by certified personnel of all high-rise-building façades has become a requirement for many cities with terra-cotta panels. Sounding of terra cotta with a rubber mallet allows inspectors to determine if deterioration of the substrates has occurred.

Metal Corrosion

There are two general types of metals used in construction: ferrous and nonferrous. Ferrous metals (for example: cast-iron, steel) contain iron. Ferrous metals will corrode (rust) when exposed to water and oxygen. Corrosion is defined as the deterioration of a material due to interaction with its environment and, in the case of metals, as electrochemical deterioration of a metal caused by atmospheric or induced chemical reactions. A common chemical that structures are often exposed to is salt (sodium chloride) since it is commonly used for removing ice. Steel composed of iron plus more than 10.5 percent by weight of chromium and less than 1.2 percent by weight of carbon is known as stainless steel; the chromium increases the resistance to corrosion. Other elements (nickel, molybdenum, titanium, silicium, etc.) are also added to improve the properties of the stainless steel. It should be noted that the correct formulation of stainless steel should be chosen according

to the aggressivity of the environment it will experience during its lifetime. A low-grade stainless steel will corrode in an aggressive chloride environment. 316 series stainless steel is one of the best grades of stainless steel for corrosion resistance.

Alternatively, steel can be covered with a zinc coating, typically by hot dipping, although electrodeposition techniques are sometimes

used. The zinc layer then oxidizes in preference to the steel, thereby providing enhanced corrosion resistance to the steel element. This mechanism is discussed below under the heading "Galvanic Action." Unsurprisingly, this zinc-coating process is called galvanizing.

Nonferrous metals (for example: aluminum, lead, zinc, chromium, monel, copper, bronze, brass) contain no iron and are less susceptible to corrosion; however, many will react with their environment to develop a stable and protective surface coating. This surface coating is often referred to as a patina when aging results in an aesthetically pleasing finish. Patina describes the oxide, carbonate, sulfate, or chloride that develops on the surface of some metals. People are most familiar with this process through the example of old roof gutters. Installed with a rich copper color, the gutters become dark brown and later green in their evolution through the patina process.

The problem with so many of the turn-of-the-century buildings is that the stone, brick, and worst of all the terra cotta were attached to the building with unprotected ferrous metal.

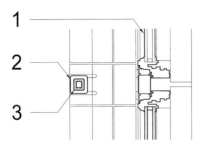

New terra-cotta panels.
1 Glass curtainwall system
2 Terra-cotta tube, "baguette"
3 Aluminum support

right Debis Headquarters, Potsdamer Platz, Berlin, 1998.

below Terra-cotta "baguette" at Debis Headquarters.

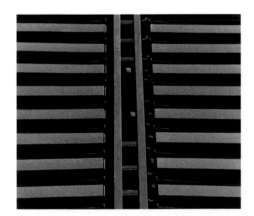

Terra Cotta Deterioration

Terra cotta is Latin for "earth cooked." In simple terms, it is baked clay. In the time between 1880 and 1930, terra-cotta cladding flourished in major metropolises around the United States. It was fireproof and could be molded into the classic architectural styles that were in fashion at the turn of the century. Thousands of buildings using this fired-claybased product, as cladding or ornament, were constructed throughout the world. Downtown Chicago alone has 245 terra-cotta-clad buildings. The Great Depression, followed by World War II, ended terra cotta as a contributing cladding element. By the time major construction projects started again in the 1950s, terra cotta and classic architectural styles had fallen out of favor in building design.

Terra-cotta failures occur with time, following a progressive deterioration. Initially, fine cracking, called crazing, occurs in the glaze finish of the terra-cotta element. This can occur as a result of thermal expansion and contraction of the piece. Moisture penetrates through the cracks, entering the porous baked clay. The presence of moisture and oxygen at the surface of the internal steel anchor connecting the terra-cotta block to the building structure allows the onset of corrosion. Deterioration of the mortar used for filling between terra-cotta elements also provides a path for water to migrate to the steel supports. With time, corrosion weakens the metal until the anchor finally breaks. Terra cotta deterioration can ultimately lead to large sections of façade falling to the ground. Terra cotta restoration can be difficult and expensive to complete. There are a handful of companies that make classic architectural terra-cotta pieces. Repair methods of terra cotta include the use of stainless steel replacement anchors. This technique insures that corrosion will not be a factor in years to come.

Terra cotta made a revival in contemporary architecture in the 1980s. Moving away from classic architectural molds, terra cotta took a simpler shape and more natural color and finish. The façade of the Potsdamer Platz tower in Berlin incorporates thin terra-cotta tubes in its design. Unlike the traditional glazed terr cotta, this unglazed material is made of carefully selected clay of higher density and greater strength than the traditional material. The rod-like sunshade elements, referred to as "baguettes," fasten into receptors cast into the vertical mullions. Aluminum and galvanized-steel fittings attach the cladding to the substructure. In the case of the thin terra-cotta "baguettes," an aluminum support tube threads through the terra cotta, preventing their displacement if the terra cotta breaks. By using nonferrous connections in contemporary designs, terra-cotta elements will stay on the building and not fall to the street below.

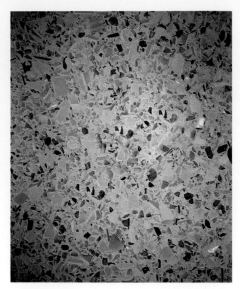

Precast concrete panels using recycled glass as an aggregate can show alkali silica reaction.

Concrete cover: The concrete base at the "City of Arts and Sciences" in Valencia, Spain, a complex of buildings is composed of steel reinforcement covered in concrete.

Corrosion of Fasteners

There are many accessory items that play a role in the performance required of a masonry wall. They include horizontal joint reinforcement, metal ties, strip anchors, flexible anchors. Stone anchors are similar in appearance; however, today they are typically made of stainless steel.

Accessory items are an important and integral part of masonry construction. Horizontal joint reinforcement, metal anchors, ties and fasteners, and flashing materials are commonly used in construction and are essential to the walls' performance. Carbon steel is the most common material for these details. Because carbon steel is susceptible to corrosion when exposed to water and oxygen, steps must be taken to protect the metal from corrosion, as discussed above.

Alkali Silica Reaction

Throughout the world today, cladding panels are being made of concrete mixes incorporating a variety of materials. The San Jose State Museum is proposing polished, precast concrete panels using recycled glass as an aggregate. There is much interest in this potentially sustainable application for recycling glass. However, there are technical difficulties to be aware of, principally due to the reaction that occurs when high silica aggregates come into contact with cement. A reaction occurs between reactive silica in the aggregate and the soluble alkali products in the cement paste forming a hygroscopic alkali-silica gel, which swells on contact with water. This form of corrosion is a well-known problem where reactive aggregates have been used in concrete; because glass is principally reactive silica, its use as an aggregate carries the same risk. When wet, the glass aggregate produces alkali-silica gel when in contact with the high alkali concrete paste. The reaction produces a swelling of the gel that breaks the concrete, causing a readily identifiable crazing pattern at the surface.

The potential for reuse of waste glass as a concrete aggregate remains interesting for economic and environmental reasons, and much research is being done to prevent the occurrence of ASR. Today, much progress has been made in solving the ASR problem, and many decorative products are available in this material. However, mindful of the Sarabond, and other catastrophes, the industry currently advises that this material not be used in structural concrete exposed to moisture.

Galvanic Action

The deterioration of one material caused by the contact with another material is a form of incompatibility. Galvanic action, a form of corrosion, occurs when dissimilar metals are in contact with each other and when sufficient moisture is present to carry an electrical current. The galvanic series describes a list of metals arranged in order from "most reactive to corrosion" to "least reactive to corrosion." The less noble a material is, the more reactive to corrosion it will be. The further apart two metals are on the list, the greater the polarity that will develop and consequently the greater the corrosion decay of the less noble anode metal.

In reality, dissimilar metals are often in contact, and frequently severe corrosion of the most anodic metal does occur. However, the potential danger of such contacts depends on the relative areas of anode and cathode. Put simply, the electrical charge from the anode surface equals that going to the cathode surface; a small anode area in contact with a large cathode area must always be avoided, whereas a large anode area contacting a small cathode area would be fine as the corrosion activity would be spread over such a large anode surface that it would be acceptable. For example, copper plate fastened with steel bolts would be disastrous, whereas steel plate fastened with copper bolts would be acceptable – the steel corrosion would be evenly spread over a large surface.

If an incompatible anode cathode pairing is unavoidable, separation of the dissimilar metals with a neutral non-conductive material is fundamental to preventing galvanic action.

The Galvanic Series

Anode	Magnesium, magnesium alloys
(least noble)	Zinc
+	Aluminum 1,100
	Cadmium
	Aluminum 2,024-T4
	Steel or iron, cast iron
	Chromium iron (active)
	Ni-Resist
	Type 304, 316 stainless (active)
Electric current	Hastelloy "B"
flows from positive (+)	Lead, tin
	Nickel (Inconel) (active)
	Hastelloy "B"
	Brasses, copper, bronze, monel
	Silver solder
	Nickel (Inconel) (passive)
	Chromium iron (passive)
to negative (-)	Type 304, 316 stainless (passive)
cathode	Silver
(most noble)	Titanium
	Graphite, gold, platinum

Corrosion in Concrete

Masonry and stone buildings are not alone when it comes to corrosion problems. Concrete buildings are equally susceptible. Concrete is strong in compression, but weak in tension. Carbon steel is typically used to provide tensile strength in concrete and hence to improve its structural properties. A simple example of this is the lintel at the head of a window. Concealed within a concrete element, the carbon steel reinforcement can exist without corrosion problems; however, the reinforcement's concrete cover can be degraded either by chlorides, as previously discussed, or by attack from carbon dioxide (CO_2) in the atmosphere. This form of attack is termed carbonation and results from the combination of CO_2 with the water in the concrete pores to form a weak acid (carbonic acid). With time this acid neutralizes the high alkalinity of the cement paste at increasing depths within the concrete. In the case of poor quality concrete or insufficient thickness of cover to reinforcement, the advancing front of carbonated (low

above and right Extension of the Deutsches Historisches Museum, Berlin, 2004. Signs of carbon steel corrosion are visible above the window.

right Paul-Löbe-Haus, Berlin, 2001. Unwanted stains from carbon steel appeared on concrete walls shortly after the project was completed.

detail, it is surprising to count the number of high profile installations where it has been overlooked.

Completed in 2004, the extension of the Deutsches Historisches Museum in Berlin has several differently shaped halls on four levels where the exhibitions take place. The south façade is composed of an all-glass volume and a large stonewall. There is only one window on the extension structure, above which lies a concrete lintel. The concrete lintel includes steel reinforcement; however, it appears that the amount of coverage is insufficient over one of the bars. In strong contrast to the light-colored stone façade, rust marks have started to streak down the face of the lintel as the steel reinforcement corrodes. The extension of the Deutsches Historisches Museum is not alone. Less than a mile away, a new Parliament office building, the Paul-Löbe-Haus, designed by Stephan Braunfels and completed in 2001, has several locations on the concrete façade with rust marks from unprotected carbon steel inadvertently exposed to the environment. These nuisance defects are typically aesthetic only; however, continued corrosion in certain environments can lead to serious, even catastrophic, structural problems.

alkali) concrete reaches the steel surface. The stable oxide discussed at the beginning of this chapter forms because of the high alkalinity of cement paste. Chloride ions penetrate the stable oxide coating and in sufficient quantities cause pitting corrosion with localized acid conditions. The low alkali-carbonated concrete provides an environment where the presence of water and oxygen enables the oxide coating to evolve from a stable to an unstable form (rust). While this seems to be an elementary reinforced concrete design

The King Building at Oberlin College, Ohio, was constructed in 1966, with similar precast concrete details to the Pan Am hanger in Miami. Corrosion of the concrete panels at the King Building is not caused by the ocean air, but by salts applied near the entrance to melt snow and ice in the winter.

Special care must be taken when concrete with carbon steel reinforcement is going to be exposed to de-icing salts. Advances in materials and mix design enable the specification of reinforced concrete that will resist even the most aggressive environments. The key lies in understanding the environment and the requirements that it places on the structure.

above and right King Building, Oberlin College, Ohio, 1966.

below Highway construction utilizes epoxy-coated rebar to reduced corrosion caused by de-icing salts.

Salts

A former Pan Am aircraft hanger, constructed in Miami, Florida, during the 1980s, has a corrosion problem that is out of control. Corroding steel reinforcement is visible at the fins of precast concrete elements over a large percentage of the façade. Heightened corrosion from the salts in the ocean air may have added to the severe corrosion exhibited on the precast concrete panels. Over many years, a building envelope can develop serious structural problems due to the deterioration of concrete due to corrosion. Salts are a corrosive element found in coastal regions of the world and in cities away from the ocean.

below and right Corrosion of steel reinforcement can be unsightly and can compromise the structural integrity of a concrete structure.

above Aluminum will corrode if in contact with wet concrete.

above and right Botanical Gardens in Barcelona, designed by Carlos Ferrater and completed in 1999. Elements of the park are constructed with Cor-Ten steel. The staining that occurs at the entrance almost looks deliberate.

below Staining of concrete walkway was an inevitable consequence of installing copper cladding on Oak Park Public Library, Chicago completed in 2003 and designed by Nagle Hartray and Associates.

Non-Corrosive Reinforcement and Accessories

As an alternative to carbon steel there are several reinforcement products available to enhance corrosion resistance.

Stainless steel reinforcement can be used as discussed previously. When embedded in a high-performance concrete this presents an excellent solution for high-value structures in aggressive environments.

Carbon steel reinforcement coated with an epoxy resin provides another option; however, some care must be taken in handling and fixing the reinforcement to avoid damaging the coating. Local coating damage in conjunction with concrete contaminated by chlorides can lead to very aggressive corrosion attack. There is much interest in the use of reinforcing bars made of fiber-reinforced polymers (FRP). With the memories of the disasters arising from the adoption of Sarabond and calcium chloride, the industry is cautiously evaluating all performance characteristics of this material with extensive testing and trails of prototype bridge structures.

Steel reinforcement may also be coated with zinc by "galvanizing." Zinc is susceptible to corrosive attack. The corroded metal occupies a greater volume than its original material and exerts expansive pressures around the embedded item. However, the corrosion product is softer than that of steel and the coating thickness sufficiently thin that the pressure is not sufficient to crack concrete or masonry. The zinc coating corrodes more readily than steel (see the above Galvanic series) and hence will corrode sacrificially to protect the underlying steel surface. Calcium chloride accelerating agents are very damaging to zinc coatings and should not be used in reinforced or metal-tied masonry walls; equally, zinc or galvanized products should not be used in marine or other environments where significant salt concentrations can be expected unless the designer has taken this into account.

In addition, there are several nonferrous metals that are commonly used for masonry accessories. Copper and copper alloys are essentially immune to the corrosive action of wet concrete or mortar. Because of this immunity, copper can be safely embedded in the fresh mortar even under saturated conditions. Aluminum is also attacked by fresh Portland cement mortar and produces the same expansive pressure. If aluminum is to be used in reinforced masonry, it should be permanently coated with bituminous paint, alkali-resistant lacquer, or zinc chromate paint.

As previously mentioned, calcium chloride or other chloride-based admixtures should not be used in mortar or concrete that will contain any embedded metal. In the case of copper, aluminum or zinc, as with steel in concrete,

Metal flashings are made from a variety of materials; however, all must have adequate corrosion resistance to the intended environment. Galvanized steel can be used as flashing material, but is subject to corrosive attack from wet mortar unless covered with a bituminous coating. Exterior exposure requires a heavier thickness, and concealed installations require a thinner gauge. Typically, non-ferrous metals are used as flashing material because they have better corrosion resistance than carbon steel. Stainless steel flashings are highly resistant to corrosion and provide good durability without the danger of staining adjacent materials. Aluminum flashings are subject to corrosive damage from wet mortar and should not be used unless a durable protective coating is applied to them. Copper flashings resist ordinary corrosive action and can be easier to shape than stainless steel; however, they can stain light-colored walls unless they are coated with lead.

above Jurassic limestone and copper were added to the concrete panel mix to provide a green patina to the wall. Oskar Reinhart Collection, Winterthur, Switzerland, 1998.

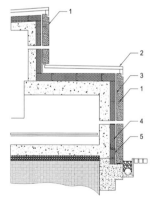

Oskar Reinhart Collection.
1 Precast concrete panel with jurassic limestone and copper
2 Copper roofing material
3 Air space
4 Insulation
5 Through-wall base flashing

the chlorides break through the metal's natural protective oxide coating, causing corrosion damage. The same risk applies to all high chloride environments, such as coastal regions; hence materials' performance must be carefully studied in all cases.

Galvanic corrosion can occur where different metals contact each other; where this presents a problem, steps must be taken to electrically isolate them to prevent this.

Metal Flashings

Concrete and masonry construction must include sheet-flashing material to divert penetrating moisture back to the exterior of the building. All flashing materials must be impervious to moisture, resistant to corrosion, abrasion, puncture, and if exposed to the sun, ultraviolet radiation. Elastomeric materials have recently met all of these requirements and provide an improved ability to be shaped and sealed at inside corner and end dams. These products break down under ultraviolet radiation and require stainless steel extensions to take water away from the building.

There are many flashing types available that use a combination of materials to provide adequate protection at lower cost. Elastomeric coatings are the most common because of their lower cost, durability and workability in concealed locations. Whatever material is chosen, a thorough evaluation of its performance in the intended micro- and macro-environment must be undertaken.

Concrete Patina

The oxidation of metals used in enclosure systems does not necessarily create an undesired effect. Sometimes, the oxidation of cladding elements is expected, welcomed, and initiated by designers. A project that encouraged a chemical reaction on concrete is the Oskar Reinhart Collection in Switzerland. The project was both a renovation and an extension to an existing museum. The existing core structure was built as a villa in 1915, with an added residential house completed in 1925. The new extension includes three new exhibition rooms that are wrapped tightly around the 1925 structure, and a link from the main building to the former residential house. Completed in 1998, the extension consisted of large prefab-

above Anchor failure due to ettringite.

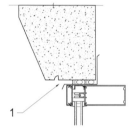

1 Drip edge above window presents etching of glass with runoff water.

Burroughs Wellcome Headquarters, Research Triangle Park, North Carolina, 1972. Exterior wall and original test mock-up.

ricated concrete walls which form the outside of the extension.

The exterior wall comprises a cast-in-place 20cm (7³/₄ inch) thick reinforced concrete wall, an external attached 10cm (4 inch) thick layer of insulation (rock wool), a 3cm (1¹/₄ inch) air gap, and a precast concrete panel (10 and 12cm [4 and 4³/₄ inch] thick). The concrete panels have a rich surface derived from the unusual concrete mix. Trial panels comprising a variety of materials were made and observed. Two materials used in the construction of the original villa, Jurassic limestone and copper, were found to give the best results. Both of these materials were ground down and added as fine aggregate to the concrete mix. The new walls have undergone an accelerated aging process, acquiring a patina that gives the walls a discreet green color. The wall details allow runoff water from the copper roof to deliberately streak the walls with copper ions to provide the desired effect.

The museum project shows how a chemical reaction between dissimilar materials can successfully add to the character of our buildings without compromising the wall system. There are, of course, projects where the oxidation of metal claddings was not expected. Other projects have been less successful with combining dissimilar materials.

Chemical Reaction

Metal deterioration can occur in any environment when metals come in contact with chemically active materials. Typically, this process can be accelerated when moisture is present. For example, aluminum in direct contact with concrete or mortar will corrode. Steel in contact with certain types of treated wood will corrode. An example of an unwant-

ed chemical reaction occurred at the Burroughs Wellcome Research Headquarters in North Carolina. Completed in 1972, the building stretched expansively across a wooded hillside ridge in North Carolina. The profile of this large corporate headquarters building echoes the inclines of the hills around the site. The progressive design has received numerous awards and has served as the backdrop of a Hollywood film. The sloped enclosure system for the project had problems shortly after its installation. The enclosure was plagued with a transition detail that had serious problems due to galvanic action. The cement stucco that surrounded the window system was of magnesium oxychloride cement plaster. The sloped glass was isolated from the adjacent material by a zinc separator. When the stucco became wet from rain, the oxychloride combined with the water to make hydrochloric acid. Where water is present and in contact with zinc, the magnesium oxychloride initiates an intense chemical reaction that causes corrosion of the sacrificial zinc material. Ironically, the system had been tested in a mock-up prior to fabrication. The mock-up testing of the system used plywood in lieu of stucco. Because the stucco system was not being tested for water infiltration, it was not included in the mock-up. The testing was successful, and the compatibility issue with the stucco was not detected. However, within weeks of completing the enclosure on the building, the zinc border had corroded, allowing water to leak into the building. The entire enclosure system was ultimately replaced.

Ettringite

What might appear to be a stone anchor failure due to corrosion can be linked to a chemical reaction caused by the improper use of

Concrete Etching of Glass

When water reaches a building, it is either reflected, or absorbed, or allowed to run down the building's façade. When water runoff occurs across a masonry or concrete wall, the water can carry minerals from these surfaces to the glass below. Water runoff containing contaminants can damage glass. To understand the chemistry involved with this process, one must review some basic concepts. An aqueous solution can be described on a pH scale from one to 14, with neutral solutions having a pH of seven. Materials measured below seven are considered acids, and materials above seven are considered basic or alkaline. If the alkalinity of a solution reaches a pH greater than nine, a destructive stage of glass corrosion can begin to occur. Fresh concrete can have a pH of 12; however, as the concrete ages the alkalinity of the surface decreases. Damage to the surface of glass can be caused by alkalis that leach out of precast concrete panels by rain, or the fluorides in the wash-off from concrete floors that have been treated for hardening with solutions of zinc or magnesium fluorosilicates. These materials can stain or etch the surface of the glass if allowed to remain for an extended period of time.

The contaminating effects from runoff water may lead to white streaks on the glass, which is difficult to remove. The transparency of glass can be permanently lost once the glass surface has been severely etched. Although concrete and stone have taken most of the blame for unsightly glass stains and etching, it is important to remember that many structures built of materials other than concrete and masonry have experienced glass staining. This staining can be explained by natural corrosion of the glass.

right Image of white corrosion marks on glass from concrete runoff.

gypsum-based grout. Grout expansion from weather-related wet/dry cycling of the stone can cause kerf (slot in stone to accommodate anchor) failures. Semicircular spalls separate from the stone panels at the failed locations. Ettringite is formed by an expansive chemical reaction between Portland cement and gypsum under moist conditions. The expansive conversion of Portland cement and gypsum can force the failed kerfs apart, much like air inflating a tire, eventually causing the stone to fracture and weakening or destroying the connection. The failure patterns are very similar to those seen at failed kerfs due to excessive anchor loads or damage from corrosion of the anchor support.

Gypsum grout is primarily made of gypsum and silica sand. Known problems with gypsum grouts exposed to moisture include softening, washout, corrosion of embedded aluminum and steel components, and sulfate attack of surrounding concrete.

How Can Failures Due to Corrosion Be Avoided?

In stone and masonry support systems, corrosion problems can be avoided by selecting reinforcements or fasteners that are compatible with the micro- and macro-environment of the building; stainless steels, coated metals, non-ferrous metals or even plastics (subject to their long-term performance). As most materials change with time if exposed to moisture, the goal is to keep water out. By understanding how materials change, one can work to protect them and prevent unwanted corrosion. Coatings vary from various paint types (epoxy, bituminous, polyurethane …) to anodizing, to PVDF (polyvinylidene fluoride, brand name Kynar), to powder coating.

The concrete industry has even developed structural concrete that does not use any metal. The new Hindu Temple in Bartlett, Illinois, was constructed with no metal in the concrete at all. This was a requirement of the Hindu monks, related to their practical knowledge and spiritual beliefs.

right and below BAPS Temple, Bartlett, Illinois, 2004. The only metal used on the building structure were copper rods used to connect the carved marble blocks together.

Bartlett is free of ferrous metals that could corrode with time. In addition to creating a building that would last for thousands of years, the temple space was to be free from metal to create a space for the highest level of concentration. It is believed that steel and the magnetic flux associated with it can be a minor distraction to the focused mind. The massive concrete foundation for the temple used a high-strength mix free of steel with a mix of 33 percent cement and 67 percent flyash.

The monks understood that metal will deteriorate with time. Inspired by the great temples of India which were sometimes carved out of a single rock formation, the BAPS Temple in

Lessons Learned

1

Some material changes are expected, even desired in our building envelopes. The color and texture of patina can add to their character.

2

Distress in aging masonry enclosures is often caused by the volumetric changes in the masonry cladding due to thermal changes and absorption of moisture. The presence of moisture and oxygen can lead to the corrosion of unprotected metal support systems. Corrosion of steel causes a series of corrosion by-products like iron oxide to build up around the affected metal. The added layer of material creates expansive pressure on the surrounding masonry that can cause spalling, bowing and displacement of masonry.

3

Contemporary masonry cladding systems use reinforcement or fasteners that are non-corrosive (such as stainless steel) or that have protective coatings (such as galvanizing) to prevent corrosion problems.

4

Admixtures for concrete and masonry are commonly used to enhance various properties. However, new products should be used with caution on large-scale projects. Innovation without full evaluation can come at a very high cost when problems with new products become apparent years after the technology has entered the market.

5

All carbon steel reinforcement in concrete or mortar must have adequate coverage to prevent rusting of metal. Corrosion of steel can lead to rust stains on a building and frequently structural problems if the corrosion is left unchecked.

6

Harsh environments, particularly the presence of salt, require construction materials (metals, concretes, mortars …) that resist the various aggressive elements they may encounter: chlorides, sulfates, freeze-thaw, bacteria, wind-borne sand, sunlight, etc.

7

Corrosion of glass can occur from water runoff over fresh concrete. Routine cleaning of the glass will prevent permanent damage to the surface.

8

Galvanic corrosion risks due to contact between dissimilar metals must be assessed during design; corrosion can be avoided by electrical insulation between the metals.

9

Testing is essential to ensure the success of the enclosure system; however, it is necessary that the materials used in the testing are the same as those used on the project. Many times, substitute materials are employed, assuming that their role in the testing is inconsequential, only to find at great cost that it was not.

10

Never use gypsum-based grout in exterior applications or interior applications subject to wetting, because ettringite expansion can fracture concrete and stone at connection points.

Structure

above The strength of a thin concrete shell can be better understood by the analogy of the un-breakable egg in a squeezing hand. The concentrated load of a ring will, however, break the shell easily.

right The load path for the Tod's Omotesando office building in Tokyo, completed in 2004. 30cm (12 inch) thick concrete limbs become increasingly slender as they rise to the top of the building, reflecting the loads they need to support.

page 109 Johnson Wax Building, Racine, Wisconsin, 1937.

Innovative structures made from concrete, masonry and stone have played a significant role in shaping the history of modern architecture. Many designs have been challenged along the way. When Frank Lloyd Wright presented his solution for the "great hall" at the Johnson Wax Building in 1937, he had few supporters. The hall was to be filled with a forest of thin white columns, which spread out at the ceiling like lily pads on a pond. The construction engineers and building inspectors of Racine, Wisconsin, were convinced that the slender concrete columns with narrow bases and hollow insides were incapable of supporting the roof of the building. Wright arranged

for a full-scale mock-up to be constructed, and when the day came to test the column's strength, the experts watched in disbelief as it withstood six times the weight anticipated. A famous photograph shows the vindicated architect below the test column loaded up with sand bags. Since that time many incredible structures have been constructed and a few have been plagued with structural collapse. The causes of structural failure vary. Obviously, a structural failure is related to a lack of strength and redundancy; however, the precise mechanism attributed to the collapse is not always clear. In the case of an earthquake, a structure's lack of flexibility can cause failure. Precast concrete buildings' structures have folded like card houses under earthquake loads due to the inflexibility of their connections. In bridge design, too much flexibility can trigger a failure due to excessive oscillation. Each mode of failure challenges the design and construction profession to better understand building materials and how to use them.

The lessons learned from past problems can help shape the buildings of the future. Traditional reinforced concrete combines the compressive strength of stone and the tensile strength of steel. Concrete and masonry are fundamental building materials and designers are constantly trying to make them better. Innovative products, such as ultrahigh-performance concrete, have given our engineers

above Interior view of Terminal 2E, Charles de Gaulle International Airport, completed in 2003.

and architects the chance to develop new construction techniques. 21st-century buildings expose their structures with greater willingness. The shapes of these structures often resemble natural forms; like the limb of a tree, the structural members become smaller as they rise up through the building. Thin-shelled structures appear to defy gravity, spanning great distances with very thin sections. The strength of a thin concrete shell design can be understood by simply squeezing an egg in your hand. The forces on the egg are uniformly distributed over the shell, making it very difficult if not impossible to crush it. Similarly, the squeezing force that the ground exerts upon the shell of a tunnel uniformly compresses the structure, unable to make it collapse. The shell structure's designer must consider the loads applied to it. If the same hand that holds the egg wears a ring, the crown of the ring can easily puncture the egg's shell with the same squeezing force. This chapter explores a series of great structures constructed of concrete, masonry and

stone. Some of the projects were successful and some were not.

Terminal 2E at the Charles de Gaulle International Airport, completed in 2003 at a cost of 750 million dollars, features a stunning, airy elliptical concrete tube structure approximately 33.5m (110 feet) wide and 305m (1,000 feet) long. The new terminal was intended to transform Paris into the most powerful air transport hub in Europe. The building's skin consists of a double shell assembly with an outer layer of glass and aluminum and an inner shell structure of reinforced concrete. The shape of the building stemmed from the Parisian airport authority's requirement that there be no intermediate interior supports to restrict the flow of passengers through the terminal. The outer skin consisted of a glass supported by metal framing, preventing air and water from entering the terminal. The elegant inner shell was built with prefabricated 3.66m (12 foot) reinforced concrete ring sections. Each 54.4 tonne (60 ton) ring section rested

right and below Terminal 2E, Charles de Gaulle International Airport, Paris. The collapsed structure cleanly sheared away from adjacent sections of the double shell enclosure.

1 Terminal 2E departure lounge, prior to collapse.
2 One large walkway access point to the terminal penetrated the shell at the area of the collapse.
3 Two plane-boarding walkways cut through the concrete shell in the area of the collapse.
4 10cm (4 inch) steel struts transfer concentrated loads from the outer shell to the inner structure.
5 Glass enclosure system in aluminum frame supported by steel girders.
6 Metal supports had reportedly pierced the inner concrete shell structure.

on four cast-in-place reinforced concrete pylons. The long elliptical tube was formed by interlocking concrete sections. Each vault ring is made up of three pieces. The top piece is nearly horizontal, straddled by the two-side pieces. The 30cm (12 inch) thick concrete walls allow light into the structure with a repetitive series of rectangular holes that pierce through the shell. The contractor erected each of the sections on mobile falsework and struc-

turally tied them together. To stiffen the shallow vault and provide support for the outer glass enclosure, curved steel girders embrace the concrete shell. The tensile girders are held away from the vault by regularly spaced, 10cm (4 inch) diameter steel struts on 20cm (8 inch) diameter plates embedded in roughly 10cm (4 inch) deep concrete shell recesses. Air ducts and artificial lighting for the terminal are located between the two skins. The build-

BEFORE

AFTER

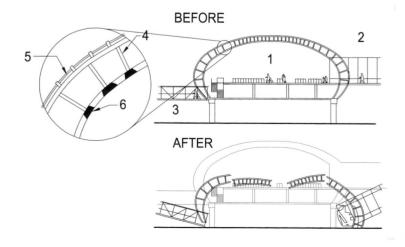

ing combined complex engineering with complex construction techniques. The concrete shell structure by itself has no internal load-bearing members; instead, it relies on the thin shell walls to provide support.

The basic design of the terminal used technology developed for concrete-lined tunnels to provide a column-free space on the interior. Underground tunnels use thin concrete walls to provide a column-free space for trains and travelers similar to Terminal 2E; however, the earth pressure surrounding a tunnel uniformly compresses the structure, keeping all elements in compression. In the design of Terminal 2E, these principles had to be adapted because there was no soil on the outside of the shell to provide uniform pressure on the free-standing structure.

In the early morning, approximately 7 a.m. on Sunday May 23, 2004, just 12 months after the terminal's opening, a large section of the airport terminal collapsed. The 30m (98.5 foot) long by 20m (65.6 foot) wide reinforced concrete section of the terminal enclosure fell, taking with it the glass and metal tube of the outer shell. The collapsed section cleanly sheared away from adjacent sections of the double shell, which remained intact. There was some warning before the accident. At 5:30 a.m. it is reported that a large spalled section of concrete fell from an overhead arch, passengers reported seeing cracks appear in the roof elements and dust falling from the ceiling. Ninety minutes later, the roof caved in. The area that collapsed was a section of the terminal containing access points for three boarding walkways. The lower sections of three alternating concrete rings were omitted in order to provide access for these walkways into the departure lounge. Steel connections transferred loads from the shortened rings to the full ones on either side. This is a different condition when compared to the rest of the terminal structure.

There are many theories regarding the demise of Terminal 2E. External forces on the building have been ruled out, as there were no large wind, snow or earthquake loads to trigger the collapse. Some looked to construction prob-

lems with the base of the building for explanations. Before the concourse opened, supporting pillars were repaired and reinforced with carbon fibers after fissures appeared in the concrete. This, however, was in an area away from the collapsed section of the terminal. Others look to the construction of the vault itself. The elliptical arch pushed the limits of conventional vault design, the curvature continuing beyond the vertical without conventional abutments other than the reinforcing steel hoops to stop it from spreading. Some believe the structural design of the building was insufficiently analyzed for all conditions of the project. Analysts believe additional computer modeling and computations should have been completed prior to constructing the terminal. The official report following the accident indicated simultaneous and interlinked failure of two elements giving rise to the catastrophic collapse of the terminal element. At the footbridge opening, on the north side, several external struts appear to have punctured the shell. Retrospective calculations showed some struts would have been overstressed. It is probable that this perforation was made possible by the prior gradual deterioration of the concrete. The second failure was immediately opposite, on the south side of the terminal. The shell edge beam appears to have fractured, falling off its bearing to the ground. Either mechanism could have been the trigger to cause the collapse of the terminal. The report also cited the extreme thermal cycling of the reinforced concrete that could have exacerbated initial cracking, and the lack of redundancy in the structure.

Ironically, France has been a center for structural innovation. François Hennebique developed the concept of reinforced concrete in the 1870s and Eugène Freyssinet invented "prestressed" concrete in the 1920s. More recently, Lafarge, world leaders in concrete innovation, introduced Ductal, an ultrahigh performance concrete mix. It would appear that the fashion for increasingly innovative buildings has strained the limits of safety in France. However, there are a great number of historical buildings that achieved everything the Terminal 2E design desired with intuitive structural form.

page 113 Penetrations in the concrete structure allow for natural light to enter into the terminal.
Terminal 2E, Charles de Gaulle International Airport.

page 114 and below The material form of Jean Nouvel's Torre Agbar in Barcelona, completed in 2005, is similar to Terminal 2E: concrete tube, with punched openings, surrounded by steel frame and aluminum glazing system. The structural form and load path of this tower is completely different than that of Terminal 2E, because of how gravitational forces flow through it.

right Dulles International Airport, Washington, D.C., 1962.

right Different structural solutions for the same objective: column-free space
1 Terminal 2E, Charles de Gaulle International Airport
2 Main Concourse, Dulles International Airport

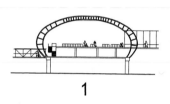

1

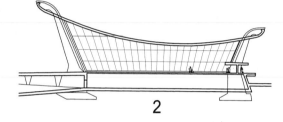

2

Structural Form

Completed in 1962, the Dulles International Terminal provides an excellent example of a structure that is true to its form. A huge concrete sheet is slung between two asymmetric rows of concrete columns. Like a large hammock suspended between leaning concrete trees, the terminal's structural design can easily be understood and analyzed. Invisible within the concrete ceiling of the terminal are steel suspension-bridge cables that support the weight of the concrete roof. Since the load from the suspension cables is quite large, it was necessary to both heavily reinforce the concrete columns with steel and also cantilever them outward to counteract the inward acting force from the roof. The connections at the "horse head" tops of the columns are the most critical in the structure. Here two different systems come together where the load transfer is the greatest. The connection consists of steel tension cables connected to a site cast concrete beam. The concrete beam is curved, rising in the plane at the top of the column capitals.

The building design requirements at Dulles are similar to those of the Terminal 2E in Paris. In its current form, the ground floor slab is 305m (1000 feet) by 50m (164 feet) by 21m (68 feet) high. The tarmac façade piers are 15m (50 feet) high. The piers are spaced 12.2m (40 feet) apart. Similar to Terminal 2E, the Dulles Terminal has no intermediate interior supports that would restrict the flow of passengers through the terminal. The load path of forces is more easily understood at the Dulles Terminal than at Terminal 2E. Forces acting on the roof are transferred in tension to the ends of the leaning concrete columns. The load is transferred downward to the ground through the massive reinforced concrete columns. The columns are kept in equilibrium due to the slab between the piers, keeping them from pulling inward. This simple yet unique structural system allows for an extremely open and lengthy span.

Simmons Hall at MIT, Cambridge, Massachusetts, 2002. Color coated red precast concrete panels identify units that span large openings, acting like a Vierendeel truss.

Simmons Hall at MIT. A drawing using colored pencil created to check steel reinforcement became the inspiration for the final design.

Each pier is independently supported, like a flagpole, in all four directions giving it individual stability and structural independence. Very deep foundations were cast into the ground in order to make this system work. The two glass end walls and the infill walls between the concrete piers are structurally independent of the main system. The great scale of the building is a factor in the overall stability of the structure. The building is kept in equilibrium by the massive weight of the roof structure. Wind and snow loads are minimal in comparison with

these large forces. Temperature changes also greatly affect the expansion and contraction of components for a large structural system. Both steel and concrete have a similar modulus of elasticity. They tend to expand and contract at the same rate, giving the system a continuity of deformation. When there is expansion or contraction at Dulles, the catenary shape of the spanning cables becomes flatter or deeper to compensate. The Dulles International Airport structure is easy to understand and analyze. Other building designs

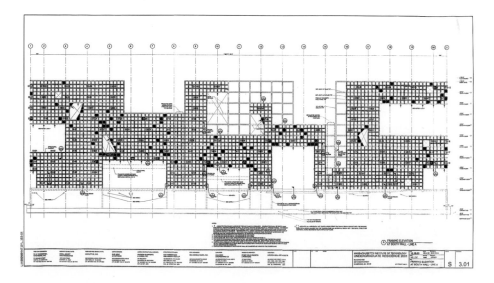

right Simmons Hall at MIT. Like a Vierendeel truss, the precast concrete panels interconnect with steel reinforcement to span large and small openings.

above and right Simmons Hall at MIT. Precast concrete panels lifted into place and assembled.

have even stylishly presented elements of their structural analysis directly on the building façade to provide a clear illustration of the structure's function.

Structural Analysis

The load path within a building structure is not always easy to understand from the viewpoint of someone looking up at it from the street. In the case of Simmons Hall, at the

MIT campus, the designers offer assistance. Completed in 2002, this large dormitory at the edge of MIT's campus is of overwhelming scale. The designers sought to diminish the appearance of the building by making it visually "porous." A second goal was to keep the interior as flexible and open as possible in order to maximize social interaction among residents. The solution was to place the primary structure at the perimeter of the building, using a gridded, precast system dubbed "PerCon" for "perforated concrete." The architect, Steven Holl, had always intended

to include color on the outer concrete façade. Initially, the thought was to have outside colors reflect inside function in the building; however, during the design process a drawing created to check steel reinforcement by Amy Schreiber, an engineer from Simpson Gumpertz & Heger Inc. Structural Engineers (in collaboration with Guy Nordenson and Associates), became the inspiration for the final design. Amy's drawing used color pencils to identify the amount of steel reinforcement in each respective concrete panel.

This graphical diagram was translated into the aluminum cladding on the precast concrete façade panels. The load path of forces at the building perimeter is literally identified with colors on the façade.

The building structure of Simmons Hall is easily understood from the street. Similar to the colored output produced by some computer software programs, color is used to differentiate various stresses on the structure under loading. The building façade appears to reference the computer analysis that was used to create it. Like many modern buildings, the design of Simmons Hall was made possible by the use of computer analysis. Computers using finite element software have provided a method for analyzing extremely difficult statically indeterminate structures. But what happened before the invention of the computers, when there was just paper and pencil?

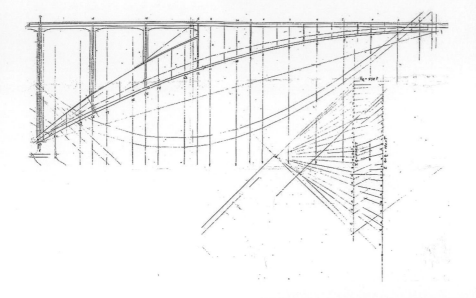

local building experience with masonry construction. One of Dieste's greatest structural forms was the self-supporting arch.

The Municipal Bus Terminal in Salto, Uruguay, completed in 1974, provides a classic example of how daring structural forms were developed prior to the advent of sophisticated computer analysis. A single row of columns is all that supports the long self-carrying vaults with equal cantilevers of 12.2m (40 feet). These cantilevered vaults are ideal for sheltering travelers coming in and out of the buses at the station. The self-carrying vault is achieved using innovative prestressing techniques that could be simply executed by local laborers. Timber trusses provide the formwork for posi-

118 119

Robert Maillart used static graphics to design the innovative reinforced concrete bridges at Salgina, Switzerland, 1929.

right Computer model of seismic loading of concrete building structure in contemporary design.

Antonio Gaudí used models of steel chains covered in clay, hung from the ceiling, to design the emorfic structure of Casa Milla, in Barcelona in 1904. Robert Maillart used static graphics to design the innovative reinforced concrete bridges at Salgina, Switzerland, in 1929. Perhaps the greatest modern masonry structural designs of the 20th century come from the work of Eladio Dieste using techniques similar to those of Maillart and Gaudí. Dieste's work was confined to the country of Uruguay, but otherwise had no boundaries. The building structures provide solutions using innovative techniques for their time and

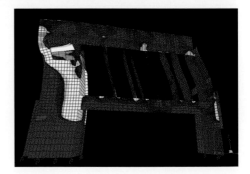

tioning the bricks on the vault. The bricks are evenly separated by small wood strips. Steel-reinforcing bars are placed between the bricks, and the joints are filled with mortar.

above Church of Christ the Worker, designed by Eladio Dieste, Atlántida, Uruguay, 1960.

left Casa Milla, designed by Antonio Gaudí, Barcelona, 1904.

The Municipal Bus Terminal in
Salto, Uruguay, 1974.

below Prestressing of a self-
supporting arch.
1 Lightweight concrete
2 Unbraced lightweight concrete
3 Prestress cable
4 Reinforcement anchor
f Force of jack
F Force of prestress

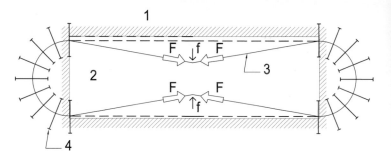

right and below The Municipal Bus Terminal in Salto.

A large looped prestressed steel cable is
then installed to absorb the negative bending
moment on the vault. With the vault still supported by formwork, the ends of the loop are
cast into the vault. After the lightweight concrete has hardened, the prestressing cable
is mechanically pinched at the mid-point of
the vault. The mid-section of the vault is then
covered with mesh and filled with lightweight
concrete to complete the roof. Although complicated by contemporary developments,
prestressing has been used for thousands of
years. A good example of prestressing can
be seen in the fabrication of an old cart
wheel. The heating of the iron outer band of
the wheel prior to placing it around the cart
wheel provides a form of prestressing. As
the steel band cools, it contracts, clamping
the wood parts together. In a similar manner,
Eladio Dieste developed a method of prestressing with the same inherent simplicity,
requiring no heavy equipment. Prestressing
creates much larger forces in a building
element than the element would normally
experience through normal use. What happens if the natural forces are much greater
than expected?

The Hagia Sophia, Istanbul, built in the 6th century.

Earthquake Loads

The dome of the Hagia Sophia, Istanbul, Turkey, partially collapsed in 553 and 557 and again in 989 and 1435, always as a result of earthquakes. A dome relies on its own weight to provide strength to its structure; however, a dome's rigidity makes it sensitive to soil movements and differential settlements. Large buildings that are located on or near the world's seismic bands must be designed to accommodate the shifting earth below. In this type of design, strength by itself is not enough to resist these extreme forces. Building designs must integrate flexibility.

The design of the Imperial Hotel of Tokyo, completed in 1922, had to consider the risk of earthquakes and the infernos that would inevitably follow. Unlike traditional Japanese construction of wood and paper architecture, the new Imperial Hotel was constructed of reinforced concrete, stone and brick. Frank Lloyd Wright developed a system of foundations and concrete structural supports that balanced the load of the building on cantilever concrete piers. The design of the supports was not unlike the fingers that support a tray held overhead by the hand of a waiter. The entire structure rode on a grid of thin concrete pins, 2.75m (9 feet) deep and 0.60m (2 feet) apart. The concrete pins loosely connected the building to a mud substrate below. Flexibility and strength are what saved the building from the devastating Kanto quake in 1923, just one year after its completion. A legendary telegraph from the region back to Wright in the U.S. proclaimed: "Tokyo is destroyed … the New Imperial Hotel still stands." Other works by Wright have had less success with moving earth.

The Imperial Hotel of Tokyo, completed in 1922.

The Ennis-Brown House, Los Angeles, 1924. Exterior concrete block retaining walls crumbled after an earthquake and subsequent mud slides.

Church of Padre Pio, San Giovanni Rotondo, Italy, 2004.

Built in 1924, the Ennis-Brown House in Los Angeles was named for its original owners, Mabel and Charles Ennis. The home is famous for a luxurious pool, artistic glass doors, ironwork, and intricate concrete block cladding. The monumental scale of the house is softened by the human scale of the concrete forms, and the combination of plain and patterned blocks. Wright believed that steel combined with concrete could be the great liberating element that would produce an entirely new architecture for the 20th century. The main part of the building is constructed on bedrock; however, a large portion of the house is surrounded by large concrete-block retaining walls that support the outside perimeter of the complex. The design of the perimeter retaining walls has proven to be less than adequate for the moving earth of southern California. Plagued by a 1994 Northridge earthquake and a devastating series of

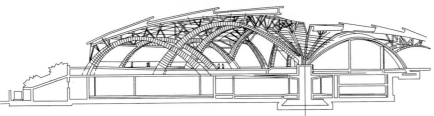

Section through the Church of Padre Pio showing the great stone arches with inherent flexibility.

storms in 2005, the earth below the retaining walls has washed away, taking the concrete block walls with it. More contemporary buildings composed of stone blocks have been designed to resist the forces that the Ennis-Brown House could not.

Built as a place for Christian pilgrimage, Renzo Piano's Church of Padre Pio rests on land, subject to seismic loading near the southern heel of Italy's "boot." Completed in 2004, the church is constructed with a structural system of cream-colored limestone blocks. The goal was to build a church of stone, yet with a lightweight, modern structure. Capable of sustaining the forces of an earthquake, the slender limestone arches, which serve to stabilize the building and to resist earthquakes, are tensioned internally with continuous steel

cables. The building's ability to flex provides a safe response to the forces of an earthquake.

The structure is composed of two intersecting rows of segmental arches, laid out in radial plan. The larger arches converge in a funnel-like form behind the pulpit. Steel struts rising from the arches support the laminated wood roof with its stuccoed underside and its green, segmented outer shell of preoxidized copper roofing. The V-shaped stainless steel struts separate and articulate structural components, allowing clerestory illumination of the curved ceiling above the arches.

The calcareous stone was specially selected from local quarries, visually examined for obvious cavities, and tested with ultrasound to verify the internal homogeneity of the block. These non-destructive tests were substantiated with selected destructive testing of sample material from the blocks. Following a careful color match, the stone was ready for fabrication in the sophisticated composite arch design. Relying on the precision of advanced stone fabrication technologies stone blocks

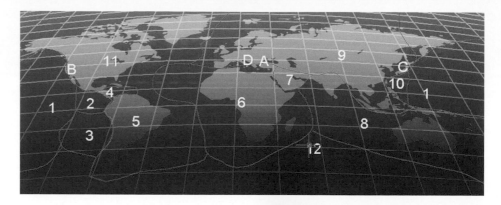

World tectonic plates
1   Pacific Plate
2   Cocos Plate
3   Nazca Plate
4   Caribbean Plate
5   South American Plate
6   African Plate
7   Arabian Plate
8   Indo-Australian Plate
9   Eurasian Plate
10   Philippine Plate
11   North American Plate
12   Antarctic Plate

Referenced buildings
A   Hagia Sophia
B   Ennis-Brown House
C   Imperial Hotel
D   Church of Padre Pio

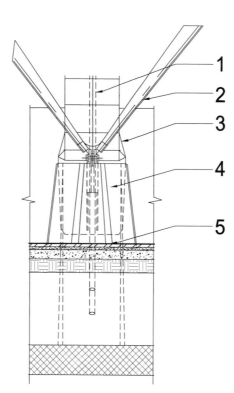

Interior base detail, the
Church of Padre Pio
1 Posttension cable threaded
through stone arch
2 Limestone block with seal-
able joints
3 Stainless steel V-strut
4 Concrete arch footing clad
with limestone 10cm (4 inches) thick
5 Honed limestone flooring

right Advanced fabrication
techniques allowed for
the large stone to be cut
with extreme precision for
the arches of the Church
of Padre Pio.

were cut with extreme accuracy prior to ship-ping to the site.

The arches are posttensioned to precompress the stone and reduce the subsequent risks of failure under tensional stresses. The stone was drilled to take sleeves for steel cables. The stone pieces were then stacked and bonded with two-part epoxy resin and a 2mm ($^1/_{16}$ inch) stainless steel space plate to ensure a consistent junction between stones. With all of the blocks in place, the tension cables were mechanically inserted. The steel scaffolds were lowered and the cables were tensioned. The flexibility of a great structure is critical to a building in a seismic zone; however, too

much flexibility can be hazardous to a mas-sive structure.

Flexibility

The Tacoma Narrows Suspension Bridge, constructed in 1940, was a graceful structure of enormous proportions. It consisted of two towers that supported main cables hung in a parabolic configuration from which slender steel deck girders were suspended by further vertical cables. The concrete deck on which cars drove was constructed between the two slender girders. The girders had a depth of 2.4m (8 feet) with a span of 853m (2,800 feet)

above The replacement bridge for the Tacoma Narrows was redesigned with deep open truss members that allow wind to pass through them. The construction of the second design was completed in 1950.

below The Tacoma Narrows Suspension Bridge, built in 1940 across Puget Sound in Washington, was the first of its type to use plate girders to support the concrete roadbed. With this new thin design, wind was diverted above and below the structure.

from tower to tower. The slender nature of this deck was part of its elegance as well as its demise. Uncontrolled oscillation was a problem from the time the bridge was completed in July 1940. The flexible nature of the bridge caused travelers to become motion-sick with its movements and the bridge quickly acquired the nickname, Galloping Gertie. On November 7, just four months after its completion. the Tacoma Bridge was destroyed by aerodynamic wind oscillations. The concrete deck was said to have broken up like popcorn. Huge chunks of concrete broke from the deck as oscillation of the bridge reached its peak. Tearing itself apart, the twisting undulations of the bridge reached an amplitude of 7.5m (25 feet) before a 183m (600 foot) length of the bridge deck tore away from the suspension cables and plunged into the water below. The collapse of the Tacoma Narrows Bridge became even more infamous as its destruction was caught on film. How could such a bridge deck twist and jump like a rubber band under relatively normal winds, and how could it have been avoided? The principal cause of the failure was later understood to stem from the aerodynamic behavior of the bridge deck; essentially, the slender deck section caused it to behave like an aircraft wing, inducing the destructive undulating motion. Bridge designers of today carry out routine wind tunnel testing during the design phase of a project to avoid such disasters. There was a device that could have saved Galloping Gertie, after it had been constructed with the faulty design. Unfortunately, it was developed 40 years after its steel frame collapsed into the Tacoma Narrows.

Tuned Mass Dampers

A tool developed to correct oscillations of structures, similar to those experienced by the Tacoma Narrows Bridge, are tuned mass dampers. These prevent progressive increase in the magnitude of aerodynamic oscillations. The technique allows for span oscillations to be counteracted by means of a dynamic damper. This was successfully done for the first time on a bridge in 1990 to damp oscillations of the Bronx-Whitestone Bridge in New York. A tuned dynamic damper is also used

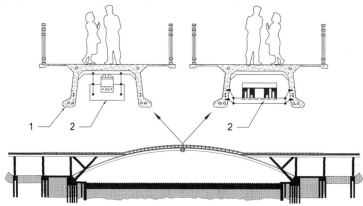

Seonyu Footbridge, Seoul, 2002.
1 Ultrahigh-performance precast concrete structure
2 Tuned mass damper concealed below bridge deck to reduce later motion of bridge

in tall-building construction to avoid the inconvenience of airsickness to the tenants and protect the building from eventual collapse. A tuned damper consists of a large mass that is allowed to float on the top of a structure. The mass is connected to the structure by steel springs and shock absorbers. In its early stages, mass dampers were set on thin layers of oil that would allow for their free movement. When the structure starts oscillating, the damper tends to stay in the same location because of its large mass and allows the structure to slide under it as it floats by. When this happens, the springs on one side of the damper become longer and pull the structure back, while those on the opposite side become shorter and push it back to its original position. In order to be effective, the mass of the damper must be tuned to have the same period as that of the structure. Hence the name "tuned mass damper." Tuned mass dampers are also used to remove oscillations due to the movement of large groups of pedestrians crossing flexible structures.

The Seonyu Footbridge, completed in 2002, provides a recent example of a tuned mass damper used in a very slender bridge structure. The design of the footbridge provides a pedestrian link from the city of Seoul, to

Phaeno Science Center, Wolfsburg, Germany, 2005. Self-compacting concrete was used to construct ten cone-shaped support elements.

Sunyudo Island in the Han River. Potential vibration of such a slender arch had to be considered. In order to maintain comfort for pedestrians crossing over the bridge, the design included shock-absorbing tuned mass dampers at the top of the arch. These limited the horizontal acceleration to 0.2m/sec (0.66 feet/sec) and the vertical acceleration to 0.5m/sec (1.64 feet/sec). In addition to the use of new structural technology, the footbridge uses a relatively new type of building material: ultrahigh-performance concrete.

The ribs of the deck slab are prestressed by 12.5mm ($^1/_2$ inch) diameter monostrands. The arch is composed of six segments, three on each side. Each of the segments was prefabricated in an area next to the final location of the arch. Diaphragms were added at the ends of each segment. The segments are 20–22m (65.6–72.2 feet) long and curved. Each of the sections is formed from 22.5m³ (803 cubic

feet) of concrete, cast in a metal mold. During the casting operations, the fluidity of the concrete mix is constantly checked and controlled. After casting a segment, it is cured in the mold for 48 hours at 35°C. The segment is then lifted to a heat treatment chamber, where it is steam-cured at 90°C for 48 hours. The six completed segments are positioned in sequence on scaffolding, supported by a river barge. The segments on each of the half spans are stitched together and then prestressed before the tendon ducts are grouted up.

The slender nature of the bridge was made possible not only by the tuned mass dampers, but by the use of ultrahigh-performance concrete, a product developed by Lafarge with the trade name Ductal.® The 1.2m (4 foot) wide deck is slightly greater than 2.5cm (1 inch) thick. The bridge's slender support structure was made possible by the resulting reduction in dead load from the deck. Using ultrahigh performance in place of traditional concrete approximately halved the amount of material required.

Ultrahigh-performance Concrete

Ultrahigh-performance concrete contains extremely strong fibers that in effect make the mixture self-reinforcing. Trademarked as Ductal, this material in its finished form is very dense and resistant to cracking and chipping. The material has excellent strength characteristics and can be used to create very thin structural members that do not require conventional steel reinforcement.

Ultrahigh-performance concrete incorporates metallic or organic fibers and is highly ductile. Contrary to the traditionally brittle nature of concrete, ultrahigh-performance concrete can bend while continuing to carry load. Its strength is six to eight times greater than conventional concrete. Compressive strengths equal to 230 MPa (33.35 ksi) can be achieved without reinforcement. Flexural strength as high as 60 MPa (8.70 ksi) allows the material to undergo significant transformation without breaking. Ultrahigh-performing concrete is just one of a number of new concrete products used in construction today.

Self-compacting Concrete

To create the complex geometry of the cones and other curved and sharp-edged portions of a building, engineers can specify self-compacting concrete, which does not need to be vibrated when poured. Self-compacting concrete was ideal for Zaha Hadid's Phaeno Science Center in Wolfsburg, Germany, completed in 2005. In fact, many structural forms may not have been possible if this type of construction was not available. The new science center is supported by ten cone-shaped elements. Resembling the profile of an elephant's foot, each cone rises up through the underground parking garage to support the elevated floor of the main hall. The main hall consists of 6,040m² (65,000 square feet)

of exhibition space. Five of the cone structures continue upward to support the roof above the exhibition hall. The building's form is incredibly complex with continuously changing geometry. The heavily reinforced cone elements were made possible with the use of self-compacting concrete.

Self-compacting concrete is made with a system of optimized aggregates, cements, and admixtures including a "polycarboxylate ether superplasticizer" which keeps the concrete mix extremely fluid during the pouring process without compromising strength. Self-consolidating concrete fills all the voids, effortlessly requiring no mechanical vibration once it is in place, either to eliminate air pockets or to ensure even distribution of the aggregate.

Autoclaved Aerated Concrete (AAC)

An important factor to consider in designing a building structure is fire resistance. During a fire, structural elements must provide support for fleeing occupants as well as rescue teams that enter the building. Cementious materials provide excellent fire-resistant capabilities, but can be very heavy. Autoclaved aerated concrete (AAC) is intended to bring the fire resistance properties of concrete to lightweight building products.

Autoclaved aerated concrete (AAC) is composed of cement-lime, water, finely ground sand or fly ash. Aluminum flake is added to the mix, generating gas bubbles that increase the volume and therefore reduce the density of the liquid. The expanded, hardened mix is cut or shaped and then cured in an autoclave. An autoclave is like a giant pressure cooker. The end result is a building material that is so light it floats. In addition to fire resistance, AAC blocks provide improved insulation values for heat and sound. Products like autoclaved aerated concrete, ultrahigh-performance concrete and self-compacting concrete are changing the way designers are thinking about concrete. It can be light, flexible, and cast into amorphic forms.

Phaeno Science Center. Self-compacting concrete support elements.

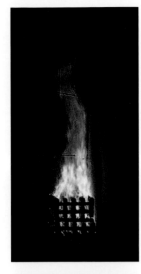

above ICF wall construction during and after fire testing

right Insulated Concrete Form (ICF)

The structural collapse at the Charles de Gaulle Airport should not restrict the way architects think about buildings. As in the case of the Tacoma Narrows Bridge, solutions can be found for all problems as we advance the art of buildings. As architects, engineers and builders strive for innovation, there is always a risk of failure. New building types and forms should not be dismissed solely by the thought that they are implausible. If this were so, our world would be without works like the "great hall" at the Johnson Wax Building in Racine, Wisconsin. However, the scrutinizing of structural solutions is an important part of the process and should not be dismissed. In France, there is a distinction between civil engineering works and buildings. However, there is no distinction between complex projects. While complicated bridges undergo peer review, no such procedure was applied to the Charles de Gaulle Terminal.

Concrete has always been a good material to protect buildings from structural collapse due to fire. New construction techniques have improved its performance even more. Insulated Concrete Forms (ICFs) containing flame retardant additives can improve the fire resistance of concrete walls in addition to providing greater resistance to sound transmission. The insulated forms are not removed after pouring the wall, but stay in place to improve the walls ability to resist fire and sound transmission. Although higher in cost, concrete walls made with insulated concrete forms are challenging the wood and metal stud wall industry by giving builders a fast and economical way to make concrete walls with added value.

Computer modeling and analysis has brought confidence to new forms and daring shapes in architectural structures. Designers need to develop structural solutions that have clearly understood load paths, and new systems must be thoroughly tested. New materials like ultrahigh-performance concrete should be used with a complete understanding of its potential and limitations.

1
Innovative structural systems and their components should be thoroughly tested with mock-ups to confirm structural analysis.
2
The load path of a structural element should be clearly understood and the effects of the environment (e.g. thermal expansion) fully taken into consideration. Unforeseen forces can cause failures in concrete and masonry structures.
3
Structural analysis prior to the invention of computers used graphic statics and physical models to predict the strength of unique building forms before construction.
4
Buildings designed to resist earthquake loads must be flexible and provide redundant connections.
5
Too much flexibility in a structure can cause motion sickness for occupants and lead to structural collapse. The use of tuned mass dampers can limit the oscillation of a structure under loading.
6
New concrete mixtures like ultrahigh-performance concrete have been developed for greater strength and flexibility. These products are challenging designers to rethink how to use concrete in architecture.

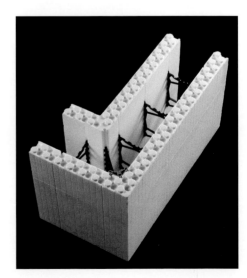

Leakage

above Unlike the Monadnock Building, the exterior walls of modern towers cover the building structure much like a T-shirt drapes over a body.

right and page 131 The Monadnock Building in Chicago, completed in 1891, was constructed with a load-bearing exterior wall that grew to 1.8m (6 feet) at the ground floor.

The Monadnock Building in Chicago, completed in 1891, represents the last unreinforced monolithic, load-bearing brick construction for a high-rise building. Towering 16 stories, with walls ranging from 30cm (12 inches) at the top and 1.8m (6 feet) at the ground floor, the Monadnock Building marked the culmination of a construction method that soon thereafter would become out of date.

With the birth of steel skeleton structures and the curtain wall, the outer walls of buildings became much thinner and non-load-bearing as buildings became taller. Like wearing a T-shirt on your body, the building envelope is separated from the building structure. For concrete, stone, and masonry façades, cavity and curtain wall construction provided a barrier method that could stop air and water infiltration while at the same time creating the familiar appearance of a load-bearing wall.

The change spurred new debates regarding leakage. Many people believe that cavity wall construction is superior to the traditional solid wall construction that preceded it. Others claim that solid walls are a better method of construction. Critics of the solid load-bearing walls complain about header courses that extend the full width of the wall section. Those critics believe such details facilitate leakage of air and water into the building and provide very little thermal separation from the exterior. Water can track its way through the solid wall and air can blow through cracks, making old buildings cold, drafty, and damp, similar to an old castle.

New construction methods are intended to remedy these leakage problems. Any incidental moisture that finds its way through the outer wall is captured at the base through-wall flashings and weeped to the outside, keeping the new buildings dry. By properly separating the inner and outer walls with insulation, the building can be kept warm in the winter and cool in the summer. As a whole, the veneer wall systems of today have proven to be effective; however, basic princi-

right Complicated building geometry has contributed to water infiltration issues at the Vontz Center for Molecular Studies at the University of Cincinnati, Ohio, 1999.

below White efflorescence on interior masonry walls is an indication that the building may have water infiltration problems. Vontz Center for Molecular Studies.

ples are to be followed, or else modern buildings can quickly become like drafty, leaky old castles.

The Vontz Center for Molecular Studies at the University of Cincinnati was completed in 1999. The Center consists of three occupied floors containing a variety of offices and laboratories. Easily distinguished from other masonry buildings on campus, the Vontz Center has multi-story windows that protrude the exterior façade in irregular shapes around the building. The building appears as if it has been overinflated and the brick exterior walls

appear to pillow outward. The brick walls are non-load-bearing walls, with weeps at the heads and sills of the panels. The bowing of the walls is not a defect, but the preconceived sculptural form of an exterior assembly constructed of prefabricated masonry panels.

The building was reportedly intended to be finished in a reflective metallic material, but due to a variety of considerations, including cost, the masonry alternative was developed. Other buildings on the campus use a similar brick material in their façades. However, these buildings have been constructed in more

traditional rectangular forms, without bowing walls and tilted windows. The irregular transitions resulting from the complex geometric conditions may be linked to water infiltration problems at the Vontz Center.

Masonry veneer walls can always be expected to allow water to penetrate the outer wythe of the façade. Composed of a multitude of mortar joints, it would be impractical to expect the exterior skin of a brick wall to stop all water from getting past the face of the wall for the lifespan of the building. In a traditional cavity wall assembly, infiltrating water typically travels down the inside face of the exterior brick, where it is weeped at the base of the wall via a through-wall flashing. What might appear as a simple concept can become much more difficult to achieve with transitions that cut through a wall at angles.

Because of the Vontz Center's irregular shape, the wall, window, and skylight transitions were very difficult to execute. In addition, the majority of the precast panels were prefabricated, making through-wall flashing difficult to integrate with sloped skylights and window head conditions. In an effort to simplify these transitions, it appears that some of the flashings were applied to the surface of the masonry in lieu of penetrating through the wall assembly. For example, the skylight transition to the masonry wall appears to be a surface-mounted flashing connected to the outside wythe of brick. If the flashing does not extend all the way through the cavity, infiltrating water can-

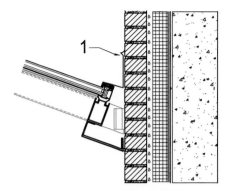

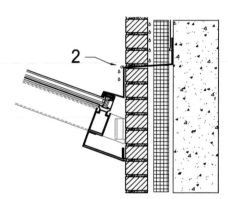

Flashing details
1 Surface-applied flashings do not allow weeping water to be shed to the exterior.
2 Through-wall flashings capture penetrating water and weep it to the exterior.

right and above Skylight flashing detail appears to be surface-applied to masonry in lieu of penetrating through masonry wall. Vontz Center for Molecular Studies.

right Masonry weep vents can be found on the interior face of the brick wall. Vontz Center for Molecular Studies.

not be directed to the exterior. Evidence of water migration can be seen on the interior masonry walls which are covered with a white efflorescence powder. Brick veneer systems typically provide a weepage path to the outside of the building. Weep vents are installed at the base of an exterior wall to weep water out of the cavity. The Vontz Center actually has an installation of a masonry weep on the interior face of the masonry wall. For any building envelope, it is critical to provide clear weepage paths to the exterior for infiltrating water. For concrete, masonry, and stone veneer walls, understanding the basic concepts of exterior wall construction is essential for creating a leak-free building.

Solid Masonry Walls

Solid masonry walls consist of multiple wythes of masonry interwoven to produce the exterior load-bearing structure of a building. Because the wall is the building structure, there is no need to provide expansion joints or separate the exterior wall from the building structure.

Solid masonry wall construction is not completely gone. Some feel it has advantages and continue to use it in construction. Critics of veneer walls claim a load-bearing structure with a 10cm (4 inch) thick facing material can limit the design possibilities for a masonry wall. Cross bond, block bond, Gothic bond, and other configurations that involve staggered patterns of brickwork to decorate walls are not possible with a brick veneer wall.

Lévi-Strauss School, Köpenick,
Christoph Mäckler Architekten,
Berlin, 2000.

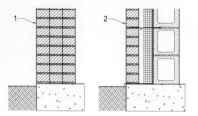

Masonry wall construction
1 Solid masonry wall
2 Cavity masonry wall

right and page 135
Lévi-Strauss School.
The construction photograph
shows the solid masonry
walls.

below Single whyte construction in a warehouse application.

Large projections and recesses that give a
façade depth, shadow, and texture are only
possible within narrow parameters for a
veneer wall. For this reason, many of our modern buildings appear flat. A solid masonry wall
frees the architect from having to deal with
concealment of the indispensable expansion
joints, and other peculiarities of contemporary
brick veneer and cavity wall construction.

The Lévi-Strauss School in Köpenick, Berlin,
has made a return to modern construction
with solid masonry walls. Completed in 2000,
the exterior of the building is constructed with
a complex, beautifully detailed masonry wall,
filled with interweaving layers of brick. In order
to meet German code requirements for thermal protection, the exterior and interior
masonry are different. The outer masonry
work must be resistant to weathering and
frost, while the inner must be distinguished by
higher compressive strength coinciding with a
greater proportion of perforations. Poroton
bricks used on the interior provide the necessary thermal requirements. In order to prevent
water damage, the bricks must be set into the
mortar without air pockets. Expansion joints
are not required, because the outer wall is
load-bearing and monolithic.

Single Wythe Construction

Single wythe construction consisting of concrete masonry units is often used as a cost-
saving measure for some building types. Single wythe construction has tried to prevail
with advances in brick and block technology.
Chemically treated concrete masonry block
units are fabricated with a water repellent
agent that prevents water from penetrating the
surface of the material. The problem with this
type of system is that numerous joints related
to a concrete masonry unit wall must be considered in the design. These joints provide an
avenue for moisture to penetrate a building

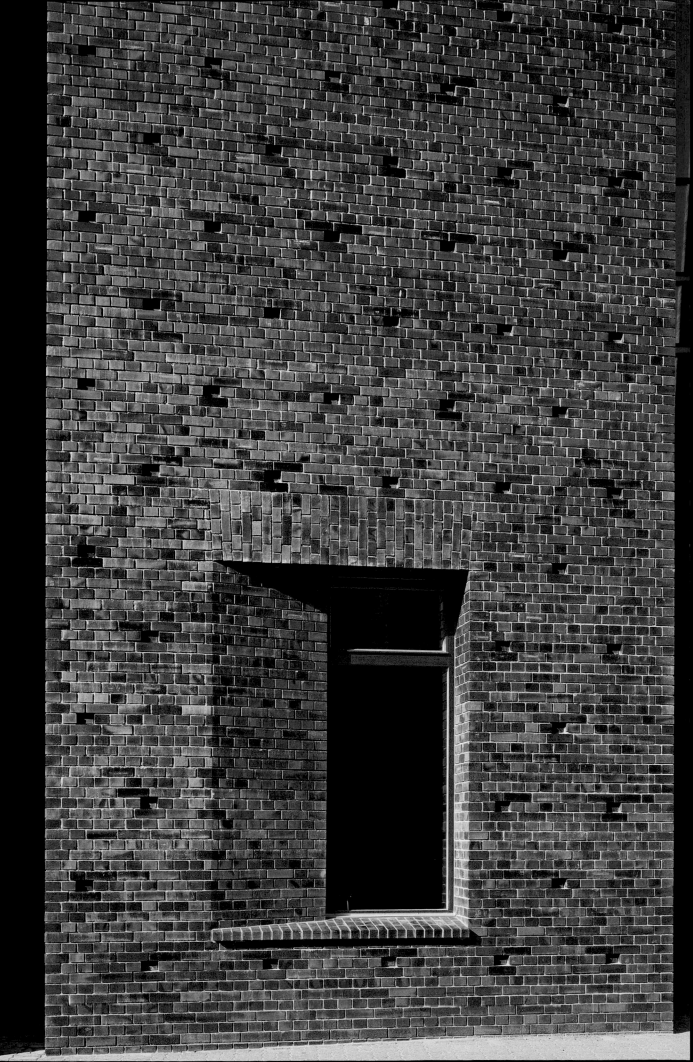

above Onterie Center, Chicago, 1986. Cracks in concrete can allow water infiltration.

right Second line of defense for concrete façade
1 Water can infiltrate a concrete enclosure through crack in the wall.
2 Water is captured by through-wall flashing at head of windows.
3 Water is directed to exterior through weeps.

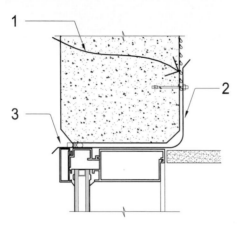

enclosure with or without the water repellent agent. Water can track its way to the interior because there is no cavity separation. Single wythe construction is common in warehouse applications, where large areas need to be enclosed with few openings at low cost. These types of systems provide a minimal barrier for water infiltration unless they incorporate an internal drainage system that weeps water to the exterior. In the case of precast concrete panels, a dual seal with an internal gutter system can be used to provide a second line of defense for preventing air and water infiltration. Precast panels can include a layer of insulation in the middle of the panel. These so-called "sandwich" panels try to achieve an effect similar to cavity wall construction in a unitized element.

Cavity Wall Construction

Cavity wall construction consists of an outer wythe of concrete or masonry separated from the building structure by a cavity. Typically in new constructions, cavity walls have an outer wythe of masonry and an inner wythe of concrete block. When the inner wythe is substituted with wood or metal framing covered with a sheathing material, the wall is referred to as "veneer wall;" however, the cavity concept remains.

The outside face of the cavity or veneer assembly is expected to allow some amount of water through it with time. A breach in the outer barrier can come from a poorly executed joint or the natural aging of the façade. With time, water is expected to pass through the outer barrier, run down the inside face of the outer wall and weep to the exterior via a through-wall flashing. The inner wythe or sheathing is covered with an air and water barrier to keep the inside dry.
Cavity walls typically have an air space in the cavity to allow the free flow of water to the flashings below. Older buildings used weep ropes to wick the water out of the cavity. However, plastic and reticulated foam weeps are more popular because they provide greater longevity. The outer wythe of the cavity wall can be brick, clay tile, concrete block, or stone, anchored to one another with metal ties which span the open collar joint. The two wythes together can be designed as a unified load-bearing element, but the exterior wythe is usually designed as a non-structural veneer. Cavity walls have many advantages including water resistance and improved thermal performance. Continuous insulation within the air space in the cavity provides an excellent thermal barrier between the building structure and the exterior. Brick veneers are used for reduced cost and speed of erection. Although cavity wall construction requires multiple trades, the erection of a wood or steel structure can occur much more quickly than a solid masonry wall. For these systems, the building can be enclosed and the brick façade can follow. The merits of cavity wall and veneer wall construction are rooted in the concept of a second line of defense.

Pressure equalization prevents
driving rain from infiltrating.
P1   Exterior pressure
P2   Interior pressure

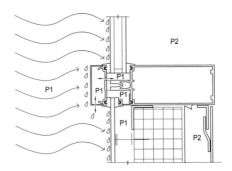

Pressure-equalized Wall Construction

Pressure-equalized wall construction attempts to reduce water penetration by eliminating the air pressure differential across the outer barrier, with a "rainscreen design." A rainscreen consists of an outer layer of material separated by a minimum 19mm ($^3/_4$ inch) drainage cavity followed by an airtight moisture barrier at the back of the cavity. The rainscreen drainage cavity is wide enough to break the capillary action and surface tension of water such that gravity will pull the water that gets behind the exterior, cladding down-and-out through weep holes at the base. The outer barrier contains openings to ensure that the internal cavity of the enclosure will have the same pressure as the exterior. Weepage at the base of these systems is critical to draining incidental water that can penetrate any of the pressure equalization holes. For a stone wall with a rainscreen design, joints can be left completely open on the outer face of the wall. For a masonry wall, pressure equalization holes can be achieved with small vents in the head joints at the top of a wall with weep holes at the base of the wall. These holes at the top serve to vent out the cavity. This type of system prevents water from being sucked into a building by an internal pressure differential. Pressure-equalized design is particularly important in high-rise

right and below In rainscreen design, open stone joints will not allow water into the building.

Second Line of Defense

There are basically three methods used to prevent leakage to the inside of the building in a building enclosure. The first method is to simply prevent water from penetrating the outer barrier of enclosure. Reliance on a single source of protection against water leakage is a plan prone to eventual failure. The second method is to screen the water at the outer skin and provide an internal drainage system to carry any incidental moisture out of the building enclosure (for instance, cavity wall system or gutter and weep system). A third method of enclosure design is pressure equalization. This type of enclosure has small holes in the outer skin of the building to prevent a pressure differential at the outer layer where extensive water is present.

right and below The Max-Planck-Institut für Infektions-biologie in Berlin, completed in 1999, has a monumental entrance hall. The brick façade, which does not weep at the diagonal, leads to trapped water that stains the façade.

construction where the enclosure system is susceptible to the forces of stack effect. Stack effect occurs when high-rise buildings act like chimneys in the wintertime. Hot air will rise through these towers, creating an inward draft through the lower floors. This flow of air creates an internal pressure on the enclosure system which draws air and possibly water through any holes in the exterior skin. Good

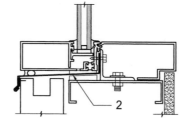

Base flashing
1 Window sill without base flashing
2 Window sill with base flashing to direct water to the exterior

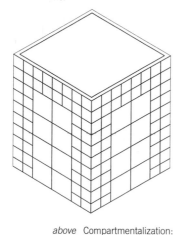

above Compartmentalization: The corners and the tops of a building are exposed to greater wind pressure and hence more rain. These areas should be compartmentalized at more frequent intervals to reduce the risk of overloading the internal weepage system.

right Kulturzentrum Gasteig, Munich, 1985. Library building with weeps in header joints of diagonal masonry wall.

seals at the perimeter air barrier will reduce the amount of air infiltration into the building.

Compartmentalization

A key component of any weepage system is compartmentalization. The system's ability to weep water out of the building is dependent on limiting the enclosure area above the weeps. For example, weeps at the base of a 30-story office building should not be expected to accommodate all 30 floors. Compartmentalization is not just based on a building skin's surface area. The direction of the wind can influence the amount of rain that will cover a façade. Because wind pressure is inconsistent over the entire building surface,

building exteriors should be compartmentalized at more frequent intervals in high wind areas – for example, near the corners and the top. Enclosure systems that cover large areas (e.g. high-rise buildings) require compartmentalization in order to ensure that internal drainage systems will not overload the design and allow water to back up into the building.

Flashings

The majority of leakage problems in buildings can be traced to poorly executed transitions between varied materials. The success of a good transition is rooted in properly installed flashings. Flashings are used to marry one building system to another and shed water away from the building. Consistent with the concept of a second line of defense, most exposed flashings are covered with a metal counter flashing over the base flashing to improve its durability. Flashings are typically completed with a monolithic, impermeable material like metal or rubber. The susceptibili-

Residential complex for government employees, Berlin, completed in 1999. The apartments have masonry weeps and vents to allow moisture out of the wall.

ty of window systems to water infiltration can be greatly improved by providing a weeped through-wall flashing under them. This added detail will prevent infiltrating water from the window system from finding its way into the building. An upturned leg of the flashing will keep driving rain from leaking back into the interior. If properly detailed and executed, flashing details can provide a path for the inevitable leakage to exit a building enclosure. If flashing details are not executed properly, they will trap water, which can cause damage to the masonry and lead to further moisture penetration into the building.

Weeps and Baffles

Drainage holes are required to leak infiltrating water out of the system. Baffles are used to prevent water infiltration through the weeps by driving rain. Baffles can be made of a foam material but must be dense and secure to prevent insects from infiltrating the system and nesting. Spiders are notorious for spinning their webs across elegant façades on high-rise buildings. Pressurized cavities within the enclosure system provide insects with shelter from harsh natural elements like rain, sun, high winds, and snow. Baffles can prevent insects from entering weep holes. If the enclosure system cavity has loose construction debris or corroded metals, weep holes can be marked by stains. The design of any enclosure cavities must anticipate the entry of water and provide a clean method of draining through weeps.

Baffled weeps are often used to prevent insect infestation into the wall.

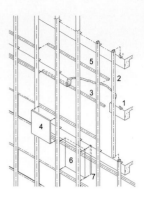
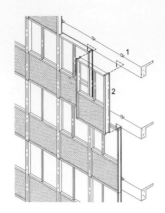

left Stick system:
1 Anchor
2 Mullion
3 Horizontal rail (gutter section at window head)
4 Spandrel panel
5 Horizontal rail (window sill section)
6 Vision glass
7 Interior mullion trim

right Unitized system:
1 Anchor
2 Pre-assembled framed unit

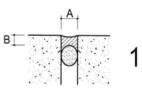

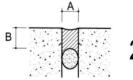

Sealant joint width-to-depth ratio
1 Effective sealant joint
2 Ineffective sealant joint

Stick Systems

Stick systems represent enclosures that are assembled in the field using individual components: mullions, gaskets, fasteners, stone, and glazing. Stick systems can allow for considerable variation in-situ. Because much of the material is cut to fit on-site, this type of system can quickly be erected onto a building structure from elements shipped to the site. Stick systems are dependent on quality control on the job site and are labor-intensive.

Unitized Systems

Unitized systems are factory-assembled units that are shipped to the site with all of the major components intact. Stone, concrete and masonry materials can be used in this type of system. For large buildings with extensive stone cladding, unitized curtain walls provide a segmented assembly that affords some of the same principles used in cavity wall construction and often include pressure equalization and rainscreen design. Units are typically modular, one-unit wide and one-floor tall, for attachment to the building structure with adjustable anchors. Unitized systems boast of having better quality control because the units are assembled with glass and stone in the controlled environment of a factory.

Sealant Joints

By their very nature, building enclosures consist of multiple elements of material joined together. The individual elements can be bricks, stone panels, or precast concrete walls. Although the exterior material can vary the material itself, it is rarely the source of water infiltration. Problems occur at the joints between elements. These joints represent the weak link in water barriers. The control of water leakage through joints is often dependent on sealant.

Sealant failure can be cohesive or adhesive. Cohesive failure occurs when the movement capacity of the joints surpasses the designed movement capacity of the sealant. Cohesive failures can be avoided by using durable sealants and by detailing joints to accommodate anticipated movements. The joint width-to-depth ratio is critical. Typically, the width-to-depth ratio should be 2:1. Sealant manufacturers provide guidelines about how their product is to be installed, and should be consulted regarding atypical conditions. Properly installed sealant joints should only have adhesion to two sides of the joint. Three-sided adhesion will prevent the joint from expanding properly. Backer rod or bond breaker material is used to ensure a joint can accommodate movements.

Adhesive failures occur when the bond between the sealant and substrate releases. This is displayed when sealant peels off of stone, leaving no remnant of the sealant on the stone. Adhesion failures can be prevented on a building by testing the sealant's adhesive quality to anticipated substrates. It is not uncommon to use primers in order to allow sealant to bond to some substrates. Clean dry substrates are also important to achieving good adhesion. The surface preparation of the substrate is critical to providing an effective seal. Primers are typically employed on substrates that require mechanical cleaning, such as brick, stone, and concrete. Most sealants should not be installed at temperatures below freezing or in damp weather. Sealant substrate contamination and subsequent loss of sealant adhesion are difficult to avoid entirely, since invisible films of airborne debris can accumulate between cleaning, priming, and sealant application. Even wiping a surface with solvent to clean it prior to applying the sealant can lower its surface temperature, thus causing a film of moisture condensation that will impair or prevent sealant adhesion.

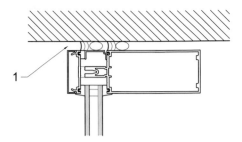

Window perimeter calking
1 Dual seals provide a second line of defense against water infiltration

Adhesion failure of sealant on stone.

right Roof flashing, Imperial Polk County Courthouse in Bartow, Florida
1 Initial design of flashing at roof transition was surface-applied to masonry wall
2 Revised detail of flashing was stepped to provide through-wall flashing to effectively weep water

Perfect seals are difficult to achieve even in a factory setting. Time and weather will adversely affect sealants and gaskets that make up joinery details. The best plan for keeping water out of the building is to provide a second line of defense. Back-up systems, such as through-wall flashings, are useful in draining infiltrated water out of the system. Techniques like pressure equalization move primary seals away from the outside surface, protect from the environment, and reduce the amount of water on these joints.

Dual Seals

Reliance on an exposed single barrier of sealant to prevent water penetration into an enclosure is the single most common source of contemporary building enclosure problems. Despite improved sealant technology and installation techniques, a single sealant barrier is only effective if it maintains its original seals. There are many problems that can lead to sealant failure – including weathering, poor workmanship during installation, incompatibility, improper mix design, preparation of substrates, ultraviolet radiation. An enclosure design that relies on single seals for protection lacks the level of redundancy required for a leak-free building. A dual seal design provides

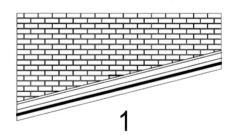

1

a continuous outer and inner seal at all transition details. The outer seal can fail, and the system will still resist water and air infiltration. A dual seal system allows the primary seal (the one on the inboard side of the system) to be sheltered from rain, sun, and birds. All of the elements could adversely affect its performance. The outer seal can be seen as a sacrificial element.

Water Damage

Penetrating water can be a nuisance for building occupants. A leaking window can chip paint. Infiltrating water at the base of a wall can stain carpeting. However, the worst water damage on a building can be hidden from view and trapped inside the wall system.

Completed in 1986, the Imperial Polk County Courthouse in Bartow, Florida, is a ten-story concrete-frame structure clad with brick veneer and clay tile roofing. With a reasonable construction budget of 35 million dollars, the courthouse was expected to serve its community for many years but it did not. Instead, it proved to be an infamous example of how much damage infiltrating water can do to a building. The courthouse was plagued with serious water infiltration shortly after completion. Leaks from the clay tile roofing system and brick veneer flashing intersections led to water damage on the interior. At the same time, the brick veneer on the tower had developed severe cracks and bulges. Pieces of masonry literally fell off of the building. Complicated by problems with the HVAC system and the use of a vinyl wall covering at the perimeter of the building, the courthouse showed chronic symptoms of "sick building syndrome" and was vacated in 1991, just five years after opening.

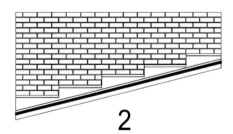

2

Although the building is an extreme example of construction-related problems, the water infiltration through the brick veneer is a classic example of a failure that occurs on many buildings. The exterior wall consisted of brick veneer, cavity space, reinforced concreted masonry units (CMU), insulation, gypsum wallboard, and vinyl wall coving. The veneer was supported on relieving angles bolted to the spandrel beams of the concrete structure.

right Imperial Polk County Courthouse, Bartow, Florida, 1986. Relieving angles with soft joints below each relieving angle and vertical control joints at approximately 6–9m (20-30 feet) on center were installed with the replacement veneer wall.

below Imperial Polk County Courthouse showing revised stepped flashing completed with replacement veneer wall.

Water leakage through the brick veneer wall occurred primarily at window openings and at roof-to-wall intersections. The transition details at the courthouse had four major problems. First, the flashing material proved to have poor durability. Composed of PVC, the flashing material became brittle within three years of installation – particularly in areas where it had been folded or manipulated, the flashing began to split. Second, many of the window flashings failed to shed water to the exterior. In most cases, they did not extend all the way to the face of the veneer. Third, end dams were not provided at terminal edges, and the flashings did not turn up behind the window sill to prevent water from tracking back into the building. Finally, the flashing at the intersection of the brick veneer and the side (rake edge) of the sloped roof did not provide a through-wall flashing. Similar to the Vontz Center in Ohio, flashing of the sloped roof consisted of a metal termination bar surface- mounted to the face of the masonry wall. With no through-wall flashing to collect water flowing down the inside face of the cavity wall, water infiltration was inevitable.

In order to stop the air and water infiltration that riddled this building, the entire brick veneer with its windows was removed. A rubberized asphalt membrane was applied to the exterior face of the CMU back-up wall, and new copper flashings were installed around the entire perimeter of the window openings. The flashing system with an upturned leg was sealed to the window frames and the rubberized asphalt membrane was adhered to the flashings. In order to be effective, the flashing at the roof was installed in a step manner to follow the slope of the roof and the masonry mortar joints. The flashing was integrated into the mortar bed and head joints of the brick veneer. All the vinyl wall covering was removed from the interior face of the dry wall and replaced with a breathable latex paint. It was important to establish a vapor barrier on the warm side of the insulation (in this case, the outside was the warm side), and removal of the wall paper was necessary to prevent a double vapor barrier from trapping moisture within the wall system. After three years of work, remedial construction costs

were approximately two-thirds of the original building cost.

The cracking and bulging of the brick veneer at the courthouse was the result of ineffective and missing relieving joints in the brick façade. These cracks were the entry point for much of the water problems at the building. The original veneer lacked vertical control joints and horizontal expansion soft joints. These were installed in the replacement veneer. In order to better understand the origin of the cracks at the Imperial Polk County Courthouse, one needs to understand the modes of differential movements in a veneer façade.

right and below Masonry expansion joints can be an integral part of the façade design. Engineering Research Center (ERC) at the University of Cincinnati, Ohio, 1995.

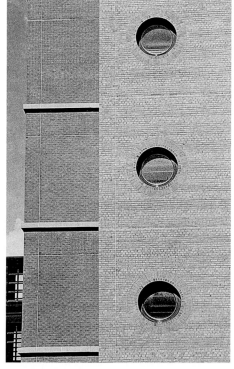

Expansion due to Moisture

Clay masonry expands with moisture. When combined with other types of movement and with the conflicting shrinkage of other materials, this expansion can be significant and must be anticipated. Regularly spaced, approximately every 9m (30 feet), expansion joints are necessary for veneer wall systems. Building expansion joints need not be hidden behind drain pipes or have to zigzag across a building façade in an unattractive fashion. They can be an integral part of the façade design. The Engineering Research Center (ERC), University of Cincinnati, Ohio, designed by Michael Graves and completed in 1995, provides an excellent display of crack-free expansion joints and supplies a grand entrance to the historic section of the campus. The stone and brick building is the east addition to the Schneider Engineering Quadrangle. Sculptural smokestacks top each

For the new main building of the University of Oulu, Finland, designed by Virta Palaste Leinonen and completed in 1989, the concrete panel joint design had to consider extreme thermal cycling.

section of the ERC and the barrel roof is clad in copper. "Portholes" and elegant masonry designs add variety to the façade. Masonry expansion joints are not hidden but extenuated with color and provide a grid pattern for the exterior.

Thermal Expansion

In the early 1900s, the thick masonry walls usually accommodated expansion of the face brick or stone cladding without serious problems. Solid masonry walls had little thermal expansion issues because the material was all

expanding at the same rate and the massive walls could sustain the force in the wall. In the late 1950s, masonry wall design changed from barrier walls to cavity walls. This new design created a thinner masonry wall with an air gap separating it from the back-up wythe. The resulting thermal isolation exposed the façade to greater cyclic temperature extremes and differential movement. As a result, greater thermal expansion and contraction occurred. The façade's resistance to compressive forces was lessened due to the reduced thickness and lateral restraint, especially at narrow piers and building corners.

Long walls constructed without pressure-relieving joints develop shearing stresses in areas of minimum cross-section. Cracks can form at an external corner because of the greater relative expansion of the outer wythe. Diagonal cracks occur between windows and door openings, usually extending from the head or sill at the jamb of the opening.

Expansion joints prevent cracks that can lead to water infiltration. Their execution is critical to maintaining a leak-free building. The joints are essentially continuous gaps in the masonry to accommodate accumulated vertical or horizontal planar expansion and contraction of the building façade.

Designing in extreme temperatures can be tricky. The University of Oulu in the Linnann-maa District, north of Oulu, Finland, is a concrete structure covered in precast concrete panels. The main building required a pale, gray precast concrete panel with white exposed aggregate finish. A critical feature in the design was the joint detail. The designers wanted the joints to be as narrow as possible and also wanted the panels to be as long as possible so the façade would appear monolithic. Larger panels would also reduce cost and installation time. These desires were in conflict with the extreme temperature range found in Finland, from – 40° C to + 40° C. Joint design must consider the full thermal movement of adjacent materials. A compromise in panel size and joint width was determined. Each panel is one story tall and up to 6m (20 feet) wide, and panel joints are 15mm ($^6/_{10}$ inch) in width. When panel joints are not well considered, the result can be disastrous.

Shrinkage of Concrete

Many building materials expand with increased moisture content and then shrink when drying. In some instances, moisture movement is almost fully reversible but, in others, it causes a permanent dimension change. Moisture shrinkage is of particular concern for concrete and concrete masonry units.

Control joints for concrete and concrete masonry walls are designed to relieve stress in a regular pattern in a wall. Designers can use control joints to predetermine where the cracks in a concrete wall will occur. The joints can become part of the façade design. A new church in Riem just outside of Munich used control joints in the façade design. Completed in 2004, the Roman Catholic and the Protestant Lutheran Churches came together to construct a church center east of Munich central. Church rooms and official areas can be accessed directly from the mutual church square. The individual structures of varying heights and the incisive steeple are shielded from the outside by a 10m high (33 feet) wall which hides a microstructure of multipurpose rooms. The expansion joints and control joints for the building are an integral part of the design and articulate the sign of the cross on the church tower.

Brick expansion joint locations for various building plan shapes.
1 Vertical joint in veneer wall.

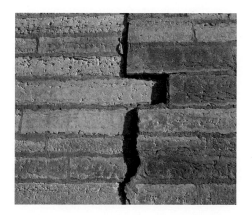

Sankt Florian Church Center in Riem, Munich, 2004. The expansion joints and control joints for the building are an integral part of the design and provide a method for articulating the sign of the cross on the church tower.

KATHOLISCHES PFARRZENTRUM SANKT FLORIAN

The most common method of shrinkage crack control is the use of horizontal joint reinforcement. Joint reinforcement distributes the stress more evenly through the wall to minimize cracking. Control joints localize cracking so that waterproofing can be applied and moisture penetration prevented. Wall cracking is not usually a problem in masonry that is structurally reinforced to resist externally applied loads like wind.

Preformed, elastomeric fillers are available in widths to fit various wall thicknesses. The shear key and flanges provide a self-sealing joint, but exterior faces must be calked to pre-vent water infiltration. Rubber control joint fillers typically have a high durometer hardness and cannot absorb expansive movement. Softer materials, such as neoprene rubber sponge, are better suited for pressure-relieving joints in clay masonry walls, where expansion is anticipated to compress the filler.

Differential Movement of Building Structure

Sometimes the structural frame may move in the opposite direction of the expanding exterior skin due to shortening of the building structure. Column shortening and concrete creep can reduce the height of the building, whereas the building façade can grow with thermal expansion. These differential movements accumulate with long or tall walls, creating a potential masonry façade stress many times greater than from normal gravity or wind loads on a façade. Localized failures are characterized by bowing, by horizontal cracks at shelf angles, by vertical cracks near corners, and spalling at other points where stresses are concentrated. Flexible joint material must be intermittently provided in horizontal joints to alleviate these stresses and allow the building structure to move without damage to the masonry.

When masonry walls are built directly on top of concrete foundations that extend above grade, thermal and moisture expansion of the masonry can work against the drying shrinkage of the concrete, causing extension of the masonry wall beyond the corner of the foundation or cracking the foundation. When the concrete cracks with lower temperatures, the tensile strength of the masonry may not be sufficient to move the wall back with it, and cracks form in the masonry near the corners. Flashing often serves as a bond break between the foundation and the wall to allow each to move independently.

Brick parapet wall can be particularly troublesome because, with two surfaces exposed, they are subject to temperature and moisture extremes much greater than the building wall below. Differential expansion can cause parapets to bow or crack horizontally at the roof line. Although through-wall flashing at the roof line can improve resistance to water infiltration, it creates a plane of weakness that may only amplify the problems. If parapets must be part of the building design, extra precautions are needed. All expansion joints must extend through the parapet and space additional joints halfway between those running the full height of the building. Adding steel reinforcement helps to counteract the tensile forces created and prevent excessive movement in the parapet. The same material should be used for the entire thickness of the parapet.

Fixing Cracks

When exterior stone wall panel expansion joints are missing or filled solid, the results can be disastrous. The 152.4m (500 foot) tall Metro Dade Center in Miami, Florida, was constructed in 1985 to house county offices. It is clad with approximately 8,700 limestone panels that are 10cm (4 inches) in thickness. The panels are attached to the building's reinforced concrete frame with stainless steel anchor supports. They range in size from 1.5m (5 feet) high and 0.61m (2 feet) wide and weighing 255kg (600 pounds), to 3m (10 feet) high and 1.5m (5 feet) wide, weighing 977.5kg (2,300 pounds). In 1987, cracks were detected in the building's limestone façade after a piece of stone fell to the ground. The cause of the cracked panels was linked to the system's inability to accommodate vertical and horizontal movement between the panels and the concrete frame. The differential movement was created primarily from the building structure's concrete shrinkage and creep, and thermal expansion/contraction of the limestone relative to the concrete frame.

right and below Unity Temple, Oak Park, Illinois, 1905, shows isolated cracks in the exterior walls even after extensive restoration work in 2002.

Normally in the construction of cavity wall or curtainwall assemblies, differential movement is incorporated by "soft" sealant joints between panels to absorb movement without introducing large forces into the panels. The Metro Dade Center was constructed with few true soft joints. Most of the joints were inadvertently filled with mortar behind the sealant face seal. The mortar effectively blocked the expansion joints. As the building's concrete frame shrank slightly due to normal column shortening, the limestone façade did not shrink. The accumulation of stress in the panels and their anchors resulted in the building façade stone to crack and ultimately fall off of the building. Hard shims had been placed at the corner panel locations and had inadvertently been left in place and not removed after the stone had been set in place. The 42.6m (140 feet) long exterior wall suffered from extensive cracking at the corners. In some

right Metro Dade Center in Miami, Florida, 1985.

below Metro Dade Center. Corner cracks in stone.

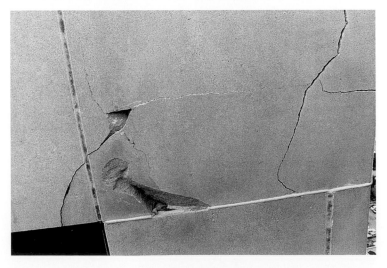

cases, the stone panels on one face of the building were pushed out beyond those of the adjacent façade, and anchors were peeling off triangular pieces of stone. In order to solve the problem, corner panels were replaced and a continuous expansion joint was installed.

The engineering firm of Simpson Gumpertz & Heger was hired to solve the problem. To resolve the vertical expansion problem, horizontal joints between stone panels were cut to provide a gap of a minimum 3mm ($^1/_8$ inch) and filled with sealant. Approximately 15,000 new anchors were installed. All of the original limestone panels were retained, except for 44 panels which were significantly cracked. These panels were replaced with new stone.

An airplane engine is used with a sprat rack for dynamic water infiltration mock-up testing.

Glass failure at 4.3 MPa (90psf) pressure test on windows in façade mock-up.

Design drawings for enclosure systems typically stay in the two-dimensional world of plan and drawing sections. However, since water moves laterally within enclosures, finding the path of least resistance, these drawings can limit the review of water infiltration weakness. Isometric drawings of corner and transition joints help tell the story of how seal continuity of an enclosure is obtained. No matter how impressive a building enclosure system may appear on paper, a laboratory test of the typical details is a useful tool in uncovering unwanted problems that could be found in the field.

In addition to following the principles discussed in this chapter, testing is the best method for determining whether water infiltration will occur on a large wall system. Laboratory testing includes a review of the thermal, structural, air, and water performance of an enclosure. It also helps to confirm erection tolerances and sequence of installations. The most common type of failure for mock-up testing is water infiltration; however, designers should not be discouraged by this fact. Laboratory testing should be seen as a tool in the design process. Modifications in the design are far easier to achieve in this setting than after the enclosure has been installed on the building.

Mock-up Testing

Many think of mock-up testing as a method for verifying the enclosure's ability to meet minimum standards of performance. This is true, but it can also be the final design tool prior to fabrication of the system. Many modifications to the system can occur at the mock-up, which improve the performance and appearance of the enclosure. In the end, it is important that the tested assembly accurately imitates the actual design and that it is assembled in the same manner as intended on the actual building. If possible, the individuals responsible for the erection of the enclosure on the building should be involved with the construction of the mock-up. While it is not possible to replicate every condition on the building, at least the size of the mock-up must be large enough to include all major elements and perimeter transition conditions. It is not usually necessary to repeat the actual building frame used to support the enclosure but it is crucial that all actual details of the enclosure are incorporated into the mock-up.

Laboratory testing can be done to verify sound transmission, fire resistance, vapor transmission, resistance to seismic loads, overall condensation resistance, and thermal transmission. The major reasons for laboratory testing can be summarized as follows:

1

To verify the resistance of the enclosure against air leakage. The purpose of this test is to measure the amount of air leakage into the system. Industry standards identify a maximum of allowed infiltration per unit of area of an assembly. Excessive heat or cold into the building can tax a building's mechanical system. It is impossible for an assembly to be completely airtight. Air infiltration should be tested before the wall is wetted. Trapped water within a test specimen could reduce the detectable air leakage on a mock-up. Excessive air leakage in a building may cause physical discomfort and energy loss to the occupants.

2

To verify the effectiveness in controlling water penetration. Resistance to air and water infiltration can only be determined through testing. The test intends to simulate an enclosure subjected to high winds combined with heavy rainfall. The assembly is subjected to a predetermined internal pressure to simulate the force of wind on the enclosure. Water is sprayed on the assembly at a specified rate for a given time period. Failure of the test occurs when water appears on the inside surface of the enclosure during the course of the test. Controlled water inside the system that weeps to the exterior is allowed. A second method of testing for water penetration into a building is the dynamic pressure test. Dynamic testing is used to determine if water will infiltrate an assembly when exposed to a pulsating pressure. The in-and-out turbulent flow of air occurring during a storm is typically simulated by using an airplane propeller engine in conjunction with water spray racks. Because of the turbulent nature of the pressure, water may penetrate a system, which would not show up in the uniform static air pressure test. It is recommended that the water infiltration test should be repeated after structural loading to confirm that minor deflections in the system will not trigger leakage into the building.

3

To verify the structural adequacy of the enclosure under wind loads. The strength and stiffness of framing members may be determined by engineering analyses and calculations. However, the structural performance test is the final check to find out if the composite assembly meets the design loads. Pressurizing a test chamber encased by the enclosure system being tested simulates wind loads. Inward and outward forces are achieved by drawing air in or out of the chamber. Failure of this test consists of fracture of any individual element or deflection beyond the established maximum under loads equal to or less than the design loads.

Field Installation

Laboratory testing can help identify major design errors and various installation challenges, such as sequencing, building tolerances, and workmanship. It is advantageous for the workers involved with assembling the laboratory mock-up to be represented later on the actual site to supervise the installation of the enclosure. For custom systems, this may be a requirement for the project. Mock-up testing cannot verify many quality control measures, which are carried out on the job site. For example, when installers are pushed to complete work on the building quickly in adverse weather, the quality can suffer. For all of these situations, it is recommended to provide random testing in the field to ensure the system on the building is as good as the system that passed the laboratory tests. Field testing is not exclusive to large-scale projects and can be as simple as spraying the exterior joinery at random locations with water from a hose and looking for seepage into the building. Points of leakage can be identified and corrected.

The most critical time to complete field testing is at the beginning of a project. Early testing can eliminate these faults before the remainder of the installation is completed. Field testing when the first units of an enclosure are installed can uncover any faults with the assembly of the system. Random field testing of the system as the project progresses will help verify that quality control has been maintained throughout the process. Atypical conditions not part of laboratory testing can be reviewed for air and water infiltration. Field testing is also important to ensure that transitions to adjacent systems have been properly executed. Random sealant adhesion field testing is important to verify that substrates are being prepared properly. These tests confirm that the seals are being installed as designed and that the sealant material is curing properly.

Large masonry buildings did not stop with the Monadnock building. An 18-story masonry

above and right Masonry tower at Potsdamer Platz, Berlin, 2000.

building completed in 2000 at Potsdamer Platz, Berlin, continues the tradition. The masonry spire mirrored by the Sony Tower form an ironic gateway to Potsdamer Straße.

The dark red brick façade with small window openings is in strong contrast to the all-glass façade of the Sony Tower. The facing and relief structure as well as the staggered design is modeled on the skyscrapers of the 1930s and 1940s in North America; however, the building shows all of the standard joints requirements of a contemporary masonry façade. With properly installed through-wall flashings, weeps and expansion joints, concrete, masonry, and stone can be leak-free.

Field water test of cement fiber panel and window system transition. Gary Corner Youth Center, Chicago, 2006.

1

Through-wall flashings used in cavity wall construction allows for porous cracking masonry walls to remain leak-free. Water penetrating the outer masonry wythe will fall through the cavity and weep out of the cavity through flashing material at the base.

2

Sloppy installation of masonry with excessive mortar droppings can lead to closing the cavity and water problems. Clogging of weeps and filling the cavity with mortar will allow moisture to bridge the cavity and find its way into the building. Expansion joints filled with mortar will be ineffective and cause serious damage to the façade.

3

Flashing details that are not properly end dammed and extended to the exterior surface of the building will lead to uncontrolled leakage and masonry deterioration. Uncontrolled leakage can produce masonry anchor failures due to excessive corrosion.

4

Flashings must be effectively installed to prevent concealed leakage. Systems should not rely on window frame construction to be water-tight. Use complete window flashing assemblies, including pan flashings beneath windows, to capture water that may often leak into the exterior wall.

5

Do not rely on a single line of sealant to prevent leakage. In order to minimize the risk of water infiltration, provide a second line of defense. The exterior seals of building enclosures are going to leak. The question is, where does the water go once it gets past the first barrier? Properly designed and installed systems direct the water back to the exterior.

6

Large areas must be compartmentalized to prevent an overload on the system. Areas that receive greater amounts of wind are also susceptible to greater amounts of water and will require additional compartmentalization.

7

Laboratory and field testing are the best methods of ensuring a leak-free condition at window and curtainwall transitions.

8

The worst water damage can be in areas you cannot see. Mold growth inside a wall can destroy a building. Proper location of a vapor barrier is critical to not trapping water. A double vapor barrier can lead to trapped moisture and mold growth.

Acknowledgments

A book that describes the lessons learned from concrete, stone and masonry problems could not have been completed without the cooperation and shared knowledge of many design professionals and people from the construction industry. I would like to extend my gratitude to those architects, builders, and individual experts that contributed information to my research. This book was intended to educate people about the limitations of building materials, with the intent to reduce the risk of problems in the future. I received valuable information from many qualified individuals, including Steve Morby of the Pulitzer Foundation for the Arts who explained to me how to make "Ando Concrete", Terry Collins of the Portland Cement Association who taught me how to get rid of "pinto concrete", and Larry Weldon of Goettsch Partners who instructed me on just about everything else. So much of the credit for the book goes to Ria Stein for faithfully advising me on the content, A.A. Sakhnovsky for graciously reviewing the text prior to publication, and to Gabrielle Pfaff for elegantly laying out the chapters. A special thanks to photographer Carl-Magnus Dumell for providing me with fabulous photographs and insights of Finlandia Hall in Helsinki. My final thanks goes to the Graham Foundation for Advanced Studies in the Fine Arts who kindly sponsored this publication.

About the Author

Patrick Loughran was born in 1964 and grew up in Oak Park, Illinois. He studied Civil Engineering at the University of Notre Dame in South Bend, Indiana, where he received his Bachelor of Science degree in 1986. He then obtained a Master of Architecture degree from the University of Illinois at Urbana Champaign, Illinois in 1990. He proceeded to work for several architectural practices in Chicago and has been employed at Goettsch Partners since 1994 where he is responsible for the design and detailing of curtainwalls, skylights, and canopy structures. In 1999, he traveled to Europe on a Francis J. Plym Traveling Fellowship and was awarded the Young Architect Award from the American Institute of Architects one year later. His first book, "Falling Glass", summarizes several years of research on glass building enclosure problems. In 2005, Patrick received a grant from the Graham Foundation to research the innovations and limitations of concrete, masonry, and stone. His studies have been compiled into his second book, "Failed Stone".

Selected Bibliography

Preface

Anderson, Stanford (ed.); *Eladio Dieste. Innovation in Structural Art*, Princeton Architectural Press, New York, 2004

Casciato, Maristella (ed.); *Stone in Modern Buildings. Principles of Cladding*, Preservation Technology Dossier 6, April 2003, DOCOMOMO, 2003

Foster, Mary Christin; *The Cathedral of Our Lady of the Angels. A House of Prayer for All Peoples*, Editions du Signe, Strasbourg, 2005

Levin, Michael; "Jerusalem of Gold", *Canadian Architect Magazine*, May 2003, p 32–37

Thermal Hysteresis

Amrhein, James E. and Michael W. Merrigan; *Marble and Stone Slab Veneer*, second edition, Masonry Institute of America, 1989

Casciato, Maristella (ed.); *Stone in Modern Buildings. Principles of Cladding*, Preservation Technology Dossier 6, April 2003, DOCOMOMO, 2003

Chin, Ian R. (ed.); *Recladding of the Amoco Building in Chicago*, Proceeding from Chicago Committee on Highrise Buildings, November 1995

Cox, Ernie Jr.; "Amoco Tower's Fate May Be Carved in Stone", *Chicago Tribune*, May 22, 1988, Business Section, p 4

Dorris, Virginia Kent; "Anchoring Thin-Stone Veneers", *Architecture Magazine*, December 1993

Hoigard, Kurt R. (ed.); *Dimension Stone Cladding, Design Construction, Evaluation, and Repair*, Stock Number: STP 1394, ASTM International, 2000

Johnson, Paul G. (ed.); *Performance of Exterior Buildings*, Stock Number: STP 1422, ASTM International, 2003

Levy, Matthys and Mario Salvadori; *Why Buildings Fall Down. How Structures Fail*, W.W. Norton & Company, New York, 2002

Lorenzi, Rossella; "A Flawed Material. Michelangelo's David Said Flawed", Discovery News, September 12, 2005

Pope-Hennessy, John; *Italian High Renaissance and Baroque Sculpture*, Phaidon, London, 1996

Impact

Fortner, Brian; "Symbol of Strength", *Civil Engineering – ASCE*, Vol. 74, No. 10, October 2004, p 37–45

Hoke, John Rat; *Architectural Graphic Standards*, ninth edition, Ramsey/Sleeper, John Wiley & Sons, New York, 1994

Jodidio, Philip; *Santiago Calatrava*, Benedikt Taschen Verlag, Köln, 1998

Levin, Michael; "Jerusalem of Gold", *Canadian Architect Magazine*, May 2003, p 32–37

Levy, Matthys and Mario Salvadori; *Why Buildings Fall Down. How Structures Fail*, W.W. Norton & Company, New York, 2002

Nashed, Fred; *Time-Saver Details for Exterior Wall Design*; McGraw Hill, New York, 1995

Stephens, Suzanne; "Eisenman's Memorial to the Murdered Jews of Europe", *Architectural Record*, July 2005, p 120–127

Efflorescence

Beall, Christine; *Masonry Design and Detailing for Architects, Engineers, and Builders*, Prentice-Hall, Englewood, New Jersey, 1984

Flynn, Larry; "Sculpture by Wind and Water. National Museum of the American Indian", *Building Design & Construction*, May 2005, p 22–31

Nashed, Fred; *Time-Saver Details for Exterior Wall Design*; McGraw Hill, New York, 1995

Slaton, Deborah and Lisa Backus; "Efflorescence", *The Construction Specifier*, January 2001

"Efflorescence", *Trowel Tips*, Information from Portland Cement Association, 2004

Surface Defects

Amrhein, James E. and Michael W. Merrigan; *Marble and Stone Slab Veneer*, second edition, Masonry Institute of America, 1989

Arets, Wiel; University Library in Utrecht, "Black – and a lot of light", *Detail*, No. 3, May/June 2005, p 308–321

Arets, Wiel; University Library – Utrecht. The Netherlands, Wiel Arets Architect & Associates, The Plan, Architecture & Technologies in Detail Magazine, No. 8, December 2004/January 2005, p 52–61

Amelar, Sarah; "Church of Padre Pio of Pietrelcina, Italy", *Architectural Record*, November 2004, p 184–195

Basham, Kim D.; "Concrete Cracking: It Happens. Here's how to fix it", *L&M Concrete News*, Summer 2006, Vol. 6, No. 3, L&M Construction Chemicals, 2006

Beasley, Kimball J.; "Masonry Façade Stress Failures", *The Construction Specifier*, February 1988

Bennett, David; *Exploring Concrete Architecture. Tone Texture Form*, Birkhäuser, Basel, 2001

Bennett, David; *The Art of Precast Concrete, Colour Texture Expression*, Birkhäuser, Basel, 2005

Betsky, Aaron; "Dark Clouds of Knowledge", *Architecture Magazine*, April 2005, p 52–61

Foster, Mary Christin; *The Cathedral of Our Lady of the Angels, A House of Prayer for All Peoples*, Editions du Signe, Strasbourg, 2005

Francisco, Jamie; "Image Seen Giving Occasion to Pray", *Chicago Tribune*, April 26, 2005, Section 2, p 1

Gregory, Rob; "Process, Ancient and Modern", *The Architectural Review*, January 2004, p 54–59

Iovine, Julie V.; "Building a Bad Reputation", *New York Times*, August 8, 2004, p 1, 27, 28

Nehdi, Moncef; "Cracking in Building Envelopes", *Wall & Ceiling Magazine*, August 1998, p 40–52

Malone, Sara; "Concrete: the Once & Future Liquid Stone", *Archi Tech Magazine*, March/April 2005, p 52–55

Mäckler, Christoph (ed.), *Material Stone. Construction and Technologies for Contemporary Architecture*,

Birkhäuser, Basel, 2004

Pfeifer, Günter and Antje M. Liebers, Per Brauneck, *Exposed Concrete. Technology and Design*, Birkhäuser, Basel, 2005

Pollock, Naomi R.; "Tod's Omotesando Building, Japan", *Architectural Record*, June 2005, p 78–85

Pearson, Clifford A.;"Phaeno Science Center, Germany", *Architectural Record*, February 2006, p 70–81

Reese, Nancy I. Z. and Phil Geib; "Danger From Above", *Chicago Tribune*, July 16, 2000, p 14–15

Russel, James S.; "Agbar Tower, Barcelona", *Architectural Record*, December 2006, p 88–95

Architectural Precast Concrete, second edition, Precast/Prestressed Concrete Institute, 1989

Guide for Surface Finish of Formed Concrete, As-Cast Structural Concrete prepared by ASCC Education and Training Committee, Hanley–Wood, LLC Addison, IL 60101, 1999

Discoloration

Baumeister, Nicolette; *Architektur neues München*, Verlagshaus Braun, Berlin, 2004

Futagawa, Yukio (ed.); *Tadao Ando Details 3*, A.D.A. EDITA, Tokyo, 2003

Kamin, Blair; "New Youth Center in Grand Crossing – A Beacon of Optimism", *Chicago Tribune*, June 4, 2006, Tempo Section, p 1

Kosmatka, Steven H.; "Discoloration of Concrete – Causes and Remedies", *Concrete Technology Today*, Vol. 7, No. 1, April 1986, Portland Cement Association, p 3–5

Sims, B.D.; "Pinto Concrete: Is There a Cure?", *Concrete Technology Today*, Vol. 17, No. 1, March 1996, Portland Cement Association, p 4–5

Corrosion

Beall, Christine; *Masonry Design and Detailing for Architects, Engineers, and Builders*, Prentice-Hall, Englewood, New Jersey, 1984

Bey, Lee; "The trouble with terra-cotta", *Chicago Sun-Times*, October 18, 1998, p 31A

Freedman, Sidney and N.R. Greening; "Glass Stains Causes and Remedies", *Modern Concrete*, April 1979, p 36–72

Grimm, Clayford T.; "Falling Brick Façades", *The Construction Specifier*, March 2000

Hoke, John Rat; *Architectural Graphic Standards*, ninth edition, Ramsey/Sleeper, John Wiley & Sons, New York, 1994

Kamin, Blair; "Terra Stricken", *Chicago Tribune*, March 4, 1999, Tempo Section, p 1

Laska, Walter; *Masonry and Steel Detailing Handbook*, The Aberdeen Group, 1993

Nashed, Fred; *Time-Saver Details for Exterior Wall Design*; McGraw Hill, New York, 1995

Myers, James C.; "Lessons Learned from Damaging Interactions Between Masonry Facades and Building Structures", Simpson Gumpertz and Heger, Arlington, MA

Olson, Eric K. and Mauro J. Scali; "Problems in Precast Concrete Facades: Looking Past the Obvious", *Concrete Repair Bulletin*, May/June 1999

Prudon, Theodore H. M.; "Saving Face", *Architecture*, November 1990

Ramachandran, V. S.; "Calcium Chloride in Concrete", *Canadian Building Digest*, January 1, 1974

Rewert, Thomas L.; "The Danger from Above", *Structural Engineer Magazine*, October 2000

Richards, Cindy; "Terra Cotta Threat Shuts City Block", *Chicago Tribune*, October 10, 1988

Structure

Anderson, Stanford (ed.); *Eladio Dieste. Innovation in Structural Art*, Princeton Architectural Press, New York, 2004

AAMA TIR-A9-1991, *Metal Curtain Wall Fasteners*, Architectural Aluminum Manufacturers Association, 1983

Croft, Catherine; *Concrete Architecture*, Gibbs Smith, 2004

Crumley, Bruce; "Why Did Charles de Gaulle Take a Fall?", *TIME Europe Magazine*, June 2, 2004

Dernie, David; *New Stone Architecture*, McGraw Hill, New York, 2003

Imhof, Michael and Krempel, Leon; *Berlin New Architecture, A Guide to New Buildings from 1989 to Today*, Michael Imhof Verlag, Petersberg, 2005

Post, Nedine M.; "Seismic Design, Quake Engineering Moves Toward Era of Empowerment", *Engineering News Record*, April 17, 2006

Indiana Limestone Handbook, Indiana Limestone Institute of America, 2000

Levy, Matthys and Mario Salvadori; *Why Buildings Fall Down. How Structures Fail*, W.W. Norton & Company, New York, 2002

Pfeiffer, Bruce Brooks; *Frank Lloyd Wright*, Benedikt Taschen Verlag, Köln, 2003

Reina, Peter; "Airport Roof Failure Blamed on Process", *Engineering News Record*, February 21, 2005

Risling, Greg; "Wright Home's Oneness with Hill is Undermined by Rains", Chicago Tribune, March 6, 2005

Ryan, Raymund; "Kinetic Monolith, Student Residences, Boston Massachusetts, USA", *The Architectural Review*, January 2004, p 36–40

Smith, Craig S.; "Roof Collapses at Paris Airport, Killing 5", *The New York Times*, May 24, 2004

Smith, Craig S.; "New Cracks Stop Search at Terminal After Collapse", *The New York Times*, May 25, 2004

Wyatt, Caroline; "Paris Terminal 'Showed Movement'", *BBC News*, May 26, 2004

Leakage

AAMA 501-83, *Methods of Test for Metal Curtainwalls*, Architectural Aluminum Manufacturers Association, 1983.

Deason, J.P., T.A. Tsongas and C.R. Cothem; *Environmental Engineering Policy*, Vol. 1, No. 1, July 1998, p 37–45

Dow Corning, *Weatherproofing Sealant Guide*, Dow Corning Corporation, October 1994

LaTona, Raymond W. and Thomas Schwartz; "Cladding Systems Against the Wall", *Architecture*, May 1990, p 129–131

LeVoguer, Brian; "Details and Execution: The Road to Quality Air Barriers", *Construction Canada*, July 1996, p 10–12

Kerr, Dale D.; "Controlling Rain and Wind", *Architecture*, October 1994, p 117–119

Kieren, Martin; *New Architecture Berlin 1990 – 2000*, Jovis, Berlin, 1998

Loughran, Patrick; *Falling Glass. Problems and Solutions in Contemporary Architecture*, Birkhäuser, Basel, 2003

Mäckler, Christoph (ed.), *Material Stone. Construction and Technologies for Contemporary Architecture*, Birkhäuser, Basel, 2004

Ting, Raymond; "Evolution of Curtain Wall Design Against Water Infiltration", January 1997, p 34–36

Sturdevant, John R.; "What Makes a Good Curtainwall?", *Progressive Architecture*, February 1994, p 70–77

Wright, Gordon; "Inappropriate Details Spawn Cladding Problems", *Building Design & Construction*, January 1996, p 56–60

Index

Illustration Credits

Antamex Curtainwall Company *16*

American Architectural Manufacturers Association, AAMA *140 top*

Carl-Magnus Dumell, www.dumell.net *cover photo, 18, 19*

Construction Research Laboratory (CRL) *12 top, 101 bottom, 104 bottom, 149 bottom*

Diamond and Schmitt Architects Incorporated, www.dsai.ca *28 bottom, 29 bottom*

Don Schapper, Aldon Chemical *38*

Ed Allen *119 top*

Encarta.msn.com *24 top*

Formtech, Insulated Concrete Forms, courtesy of Kevin Grogan *129*

The Frank Lloyd Wright Foundation, Taliesin West, Scottsdale, AZ *121 bottom*

Getty Images *111 top*

Steve Hall, Hedrich Blessing, www.hedrichblessing.com, courtesy of Ross Barney + Jankowski Inc Architects *27 top*

Illustration redrawn from detail on page 11-2 and page 5-3 of Ian R. Chin; *Recladding of the Amoco Building in Chicago*, Proceeding from Chicago Committee on Highrise Buildings, November 1995 *12, 14 top*

Jan Bitter courtesy of Jan Bitter Fotografie www.janbitter.de *58 top and bottom right*

James Steincamp, James@Steincampphotography.com *32 bottom, 34 top*

Johnson Architectural Images, AJ1507; © Artifice Inc. *108 bottom*

Lisa Krichilsky *21*

Kevin A. O'Connor, AIA, Ross Barney + Jankowski Inc Architects *26, 27 bottom*

Kim Zwarts (design of pattern on precast mould at University Library Utrecht) *58 bottom right*

Léon Wohlhage Wernik Architekten *64*

Galvin Loughran *71, 84*

Liam Loughran *57 bottom*

Mary Margaret Loughran *95, 102 top, 104 middle, 114, 115 bottom*

Mike Giso *17 bottom left and bottom right*

Nabih Youssef Associates *118 bottom*

Nicholas Stanos *20 middle*

Oklahoma Publishing Company (OPUBCO) www.newsok.com *24 bottom*

O'Mally Creadon Productions *122 top*

Pavlo Berko *87 bottom*

Pennie Sabel, courtesy of Building Stone Institute *13 bottom, 14 bottom, 16, 17 top, 124 middle right*

Philippe Rualt, courtesy of Remy Marciano Architecte DPLG *78*

Pulitzer Foundation *68, 69 top*

Jay Williams, AIA *116 top, 117 top*

John Ronan Architect *88 top*

Randy Chapple AIA *90 top*

R. Van Petten AIA *94*

Scott Seyer AIA *9, 10 right, 11* (photo rendering of 300 east Randolph Expansion)

Simpson Gumpertz & Heger Inc. *116 bottom, 117 bottom middle, 148*

Shutterstock.com *10, 15, 20 top, 22, 32 top, 51 top, 70 top, 73 top, 76 top, 82 left, 86 bottom, 110 top, 113, 121 top, 125*

Stanford Anderson (ed.) *Eladio Dieste. Innovation in Structural Art 118 top, 119 top, 120*

Tim Griffith, www.timgriffith.com, courtesy of Diamond and Schmitt Architects Inc. *28 top, 29 top*

Travis Soberg *48 left*

Wiel Arets Architects *58 bottom left*

Virta Palaste Leinonen Architects *144*

Ductal *126 top*

Stefan Müller, courtesy of Christoph Mäckler Architekten *135*

Christoph Mäckler Architekten *134 bottom right*

ArkHouse Architects *80*

Illustration redrawn from Christine Beall; *Masonry Design and Detailing, For Architects, Engineers, and Builders*, Prentice-Hall, Englewood, New Jersey 1984 *36, 46 bottom left, 47 left*

Illustration redrawn from detail on page 187 of Günter Pfeifer and Antje M. Liebers, Per Brauneck, *Exposed Concrete. Technology and Design*, Birkhäuser, Basel, 2005 *56 left*

Illustration redrawn from detail on page 406 and page 187 of Christine Beall; *Masonry Design and Detailing for Architects, Engineers, and Builders*, Prentice-Hall, Englewood, New Jersey 1984 *46 bottom and 47 left*

Image redrawn from detail on page 64 of James E. Amrhein and Michael W. Merrigan; *Marble and Stone Slab Veneer*, second edition, Masonry Institute of America, 1989 *20*

Image redrawn from detail on page 262 of Matthys Levy and Mario Salvadori; *Why Buildings Fall Down. How Structures Fail*, W.W. Norton & Company, New York, 2002 *25*

Image redrawn from detail on page 31A of Lee Bey; "The trouble with terra-cotta", *Chicago Sun-Times*, October 18, 1998 *96*

Image redrawn from detail on page 31 of *Indiana Limestone Handbook*, Indiana Limestone Institute of America, 2000 *45*

Images redrawn from the information on the website of the Renzo Piano Building Workshop, www.renzopiano.com *36 bottom, 37 bottom*

All other illustrations were provided by the author.

Graphic design: Gabrielle Pfaff, Berlin
Engineering review and copy editing: Richard Palmer,
Palmer Consulting, Divonne-les-Bains, France

A CIP catalogue record for this book is available from
the Library of Congress, Washington D.C., USA

Bibliographic information published by Die Deutsche
Bibliothek
Die Deutsche Bibliothek lists this publication in the
Deutsche Nationalbibliografie; detailed bibliographic
data is available in the internet at http://dnb.ddb.de.

© 2007 Birkhäuser – Publishers for Architecture,
P.O. Box 133, CH-4010 Basel, Switzerland
Part of Springer Science+Business Media
Printed on acid-free paper produced from chlorine-
free pulp. TCF ∞

Printed in Germany
ISBN-13: 978-3-7643-7329-0
ISBN-10: 3-7643-7329-6

http://www.birkhauser.ch

9 8 7 6 5 4 3 2 1

Front cover: Detail of Finlandia Hall, Helsinki